Second Language Classroom Research
Issues and Opportunities

Second Language Research:
Theoretical and Methodological Issues
Jacquelyn Schachter and Susan Gass, Editors

Tarone/Gass/Cohen ● Research Methodology in
Second-Language Acquisition

Schachter/Gass ● Second Language
Classroom Research:
Issues and Opportunities

Second Language Classroom Research
Issues and Opportunities

Edited by

Jacquelyn Schachter
University of Oregon

Susan Gass
Michigan State University

LEA LAWRENCE ERLBAUM ASSOCIATES, PUBLISHERS
1996 Mahwah, New Jersey

Lawrence Erlbaum Associates, Inc., Publishers
10 Industrial Avenue
Mahwah, NJ 07430

Cover design by Gail Silverman

Library of Congress Cataloging-in-Publication Data

Second language classroom research : issues and opportunities / edited
by Jacquelyn Schachter, Susan Gass.
        p.   cm.
Includes bibliographical references and index.
ISBN 0-8058-1935-5 (alk. paper). — ISBN 0-8058-1936-3 (pbk. : alk. paper)
1. Language and languages—Study and teaching—Research.
2. Second language acquisition—Research.   I. Schachter, Jacquelyn.
II. Gass, Susan M.
P53.S385   1996
418'.007—dc20   96-829
                                                     CIP

Books published by Lawrence Erlbaum Associates are printed on acid-free paper, and their bindings are chosen for strength and durability.

Printed in the United States of America
10 9 8 7 6 5 4 3 2 1

Contents

Introduction

Jacquelyn Schachter
University of Oregon

Susan Gass
Michigan State University

As directors (one former and one current) of language institutes housed within academic units of large public universities, we have for a long time been concerned with the issue of conducting research projects within our respective centers. Approximately 3 years ago, together with Patsy Lightbown, we found ourselves in a rare situation: We had several uninterrupted hours to talk! We were going by car from Eugene, Oregon, where we had attended a cognitive science and SLA conference, to Seattle, Washington, where we were about to attend an American Association for Applied Linguistics (AAAL) meeting. Given Patsy Lightbown's long experience in conducting research within school settings, we decided to get her to talk about the nitty-gritty of doing classroom-based research. We were interested in neither the generation of research questions nor the setting up of research projects, for we had had much experience in that area. Rather, we wanted an honest behind-the-scenes look at what happens from the beginning to the end of a research project within a classroom context. In other words, we did not want to know about the "end result," the part that appears on the printed pages of journals. Rather, we wanted to know about the process that lay behind those printed pages; the good, the bad and the ugly.

Patsy was most helpful in getting us to think about the myriad steps that must be taken in making a classroom research project successful. She gave us an earful. Reports of research projects make it all look so simple. The methodology sections of published papers states who the subjects were and what they did. There is no indication of the blood, sweat, and tears that go into getting permission to undertake the project, that go into actual data collection, that go into transcription, and so forth. At the AAAL conference, we met and talked with Margaret Early, another experienced classroom-based researcher. She gave us another earful. We were considerably enlightened. But then we began to think. Shouldn't we warn our graduate students about some of the pitfalls before sending them off into the world of classroom-based data collection? Shouldn't we share this new awareness with other SLA researchers? At that conference, a symposium was planned for a subsequent conference (1994) and the seed for this book was planted.

In talking about these issues in the following years, we became acutely aware that the books that deal with classroom research do little to help researchers and future researchers understand the complexities and the problematics of conducting classroom-based research. Journals in the field of second language learning and teaching are filled with reports of studies conducted with learners and teachers in a classroom context. The research is described, analyzed, and synthesized with relevant conclusions being drawn. In a sense, reading the journal reports is much like going to the professional theater—it all looks so easy, so professional. We may disagree with the interpretation, we may disagree with some of the underlying assumptions on which the studies were based, we may even disagree with the way the research was conducted. However, we rarely think about what has gone on behind the scenes as authors come up with the report—a professional production or publication. This book, then, is an attempt to remedy that shortcoming and is seen as a complement to the books already in existence on classroom research.

The book is intended to give a "no holds barred" look at how some scholars have viewed their research projects and, in that sense, give the reader an understanding of the numerous considerations, decisions, and compromises that need to be made in the course of conceptualizing, designing, and conducting classroom research. As Duff and Early point out in their chapter, the very word "problematics" suggests some negativity in conducting research. Perhaps it is better to think of some of the so-called problems or compromises as part of a natural evolution. Certainly, if we expect something to occur, and are prepared for it, we are less likely to view it as problematic. This book is intended as a step in that process.

The chapters cover a wide variety of topics and a wide range of research sites. Thus, the book includes research conducted in elementary and secondary school settings and in university settings; it includes research conducted in the United States, in Canada, and in Europe; it includes research conducted by predissertation graduate students, by doctoral candidates, and by senior scholars.

The first three chapters deal with issues faced by the authors as they attempted to conduct research projects within school settings. In the chapter by Duff and Early, the authors point to similarities in the difficulties and challenges they faced independently while conducting research on two continents (Early in Canada and Duff in Hungary). In the first case, the research involved immigrant and minority children and, in particular, the meshing of language and content within the schools. The second case was concerned with English as a Foreign Language (EFL) programs in dual-language schools in Hungary. What emerges from their chapter is strong motivation for having a flexible agenda when undertaking research of the sort they describe, because the goals at the outset of the project often need to be modified to fit the exigencies of time, place, and individuals. This may necessitate a reexamination of the criteria involved in both quantitative and qualitative methodologies. Highlighted here is the need to recognize that the researchers are not alone in the process; there are multiple stakeholders (not the least of whom are the children), all of whom have their own concerns (personal, institutional and/or sociopolitical). They conclude their chapter with a discussion of the factors that became apparent to them during the course of the research and that were crucial in the researchers' eventual successes.

The chapter by Spada, Ranta, and Lightbown also describes research undertaken in a school setting, and like the research discussed by Early in chapter 1, it was conducted in Canada. The students in this study, however, were Francophone children (grades 5 and 6) learning English in intensive English programs. As in other chapters in this volume, the authors stress the necessity of establishing relationships and feelings of trust with the teachers whose classes are being observed. They discuss ways in which they accomplished this in their settings, not the least of which was extensive observation of the classes prior to any "real" data collection. They also point to the necessity of providing sufficient instruction to teachers as to how experimental materials should be used (see also Kuiper & Plough) and to the need for debriefing teachers (see also Polio) at the end of the research.

Rounds turns to the anthropological literature as a framework for discussing her research, which took place in an immersion program in a local elementary school in her community. She had been approached by the school district to undertake research and, as a result, conducted a graduate seminar during which she supervised the graduate students undertaking research in this school setting. She chronicles the preparation that she and her students engaged in, the questions they planned to ask, and then the brick wall they hit in the midst of the project, when one particular teacher's agenda did not mesh with theirs. In her chapter, she compares the work she and her students were doing with that of an anthropological fieldworker who was taking his or her equipment to a new place with the goal of describing the new place so that others could understand it. This chapter provides an excellent reminder to those conducting research that we are guests in someone else's territory and that others may feel uncomfortable and lack trust and confidence in what we are doing. Unless an appropriate atmosphere is established a priori, those whose classrooms we visit may feel threatened and may react by questioning the appropriateness of the entire project.

Polio discusses a series of research projects conducted while she was a predissertation graduate student. Her focus in this research (conducted with Patsy Duff) was on the use or nonuse of the target language in foreign language classrooms in a large public U.S. research university. She describes research paradigms (quantitative and qualitative), focusing on problems associated with each, labeling her own research ethnographic. Like others in this book, Polio acknowledges the difficulty of locating a cooperative teacher, but more important is the recognition of the difficulty inherent in writing up the results of a descriptive study such as this one without identifying the teacher (whose behaviors may or may not be pedagogically sound or even in accord with those of the program within which she or he is teaching). This, of course, is a crucial issue for all research in which there are only a few teachers involved, or in which the identification of a teacher by virtue of some particular characteristic is possible. In discussing these issues, Polio makes suggestions about how they can be sensitively dealt with (e.g., acknowledging the teacher's point of view and the realities of the classroom, debriefing teachers, eliciting and publishing suggestions and teaching philosophies or techniques from teachers).

Like Rounds, who draws on an anthropological perspective to understand her research experience, Kuiper and Plough also look to another field to understand theirs. They, however, turn to the field of sociology and to the notion of communicative networks in order to make sense of the ways in which the research described was successful and the ways in which it was not. This chapter is unique in that it brings together two perspectives on the same research project; one is that of the author who was conducting doctoral research, and the other is that of a teacher and assistant to the coordinator of the language program in which the research was conducted. The focus in this chapter is on the necessity of establishing an environment that allows the development of critical interpersonal relationships. They posit a model to help understand the important relationships in the research project under consideration, a model which is network based rather than hierarchically organized. They argue that this conceptualization of a research project situated in a university context helps a researcher place himself or herself in a way that most effectively allows the work to be carried out harmoniously and with full consideration of all players.

The chapter by Rounds and Schachter also describes research conducted within a university context. The project was initially conceived of within the context of a graduate seminar in which the focus was learning outcomes of explicit teaching of grammatical structures. In order to investigate this issue, concepts from a wide range of fields needed to be brought together (psychology, linguistics, second language acquisition, and pedagogy). Their chapter recounts the development from an initial idea to a full-blown research project. They point out the challenge of being constrained by a number of disciplines and by the practical concern that the research project be suitable and appropriate for an already existing ESL program. In their chapter they establish the concept of screens through which the research project had to pass, including the theoretical, practical, and institutional. They describe their ups and downs, how they went about discarding ideas before finally coming up with a viable project, and the recognition of the human side of researchers themselves, as well as of teachers and learners. This chapter is clearly an eye opener, laying out for the reader the complexities of the design phase behind a well thought out research project.

Markee's chapter describes work that is also situated within the context of a large public university; its focus is on action research and on ways of involving graduate students in that research. The author shows the links that can be made between second language classroom research and a "diffusion of innovations" perspective on managing educational change. In the first part of the chapter, Markee outlines how second language classroom research may contribute to implementing social change by describing a framework that allows us to understand different ways in which knowledge may be constructed and utilized. In the second part, he discusses the practical problems encountered in the process of trying to institutionalize action research by ESL teaching assistants at a research university. He further outlines the solutions that he and his students devised and discusses the relative successes and failures of these solutions.

Larsen-Freeman brings many of the issues together in her final summary chapter. She discusses seven issues that emerge from earlier chapters: problems, place, purpose, particularizability, participants, power, and perspectives. An interesting discussion here has to do with the notion of problems, which Duff and Early suggest is an overly negative way of looking at issues involved in classroom research. Larsen-Freeman argues that some of the difficulties discussed with regard to classroom research may be a function of the kind of research that is being conducted, that is, qualitative research. As researchers in a field, we are not yet sure enough of ourselves in undertaking this kind of research; we do not have well-defined and well-established paradigms within which we can work. Hence, "difficulties" are seen as problems when perhaps they would be better viewed as natural steps in the development of a field and of a research paradigm. In thinking about all of the issues that Larsen-Freeman identifies, one is awed by the complexities of the classroom, but also challenged by them.

The chapters in this volume exhibit remarkable similarities in their discussions of certain issues arising from classroom research. Primary among these issues is the need to recognize often competing agendas of participants ("multiple stakeholders," to use a phrase from the Duff & Early chapter), as well as to determine who the participants are. That is, the definition of participant is expanded to include not only the immediate visible participants, such as teacher, researcher, and student, but also more indirectly related participants such as ministries of education, funding agencies, school boards, and so forth. Second is the notion of change. From the inception of a project to its conclusion, contexts and agendas often change before a researcher's eyes adjust to the original context and agenda. This often demands flexibility in resetting research goals. A third issue is the need for a harmonious and trusting relationship among all participants. Although this may greatly affect the timetable of a project, the payoff comes at the end, and in the possibility of future projects.

A further ethical dilemma confronts everyone conducting classroom-based research: Has the "publish or perish" notion so prevalent in North American universities interfered with the quality of classroom-based research? Is it possible to conduct classroom projects that take into account their multifaceted nature and their inevitable delays, and still publish the requisite amount to hold onto our jobs, and receive raises and promotions? We believe the answer is a resounding "yes," simply because data from such projects are so rich, so intriguing. It is probable, however, that within academic institutions, there will be a need to reconsider the evaluation criteria for research. Collaborative research, timetables, and so forth may have to be rethought if the kind of research that is described in many of the chapters of this book is to be encouraged. Although the chapters in this volume did not deal with this issue, it is a further and competing agenda of which we must be cognizant.

The authors of the chapters in this book deserve credit in that they have laid their cards on the table, giving us a behind-the-scenes look at difficult ethical decisions and at the messiness and disorder of their research projects. We hope that these behind-the-scenes glimpses will be useful to researchers as they contemplate the vagaries and potential pitfalls of undertaking research in a second language classroom. We further hope that by exposing the difficulties of conducting research of this sort, other researchers will be better equipped to consider the process of research just as important as the eventual product. We firmly believe that by valuing the process along with the product, the community (in the broadest sense) will be the ultimate beneficiary.

Chapter 1

Problematics of Classroom Research Across Sociopolitical Contexts[1]

Patricia Duff
Margaret Early
University of British Columbia

This chapter examines some of the problematic features of conducting classroom-based research in the field of applied linguistics. To illustrate the complexity of implementing projects, two long-term studies conducted in Canada and Hungary are presented. The Canadian research was concerned with the education of immigrant and minority children in one large urban center, and with methods of integrating language and content instruction in particular. Both elementary and secondary schools have been involved in this study from 1987 to the present. The Hungarian research was situated in dual-language (late immersion) secondary schools in three Hungarian cities from 1989 to 1992. Its objectives were to document learners' progress in English as a foreign language (EFL) as well as in their academic subjects, and to investigate changing language socialization practices in content classrooms. Remarkably

---

[1] This is a revised version of papers presented at the 10th World Congress of the International Association of Applied Linguistics, August 10, 1993 and the American Association for Applied Linguistics, Baltimore, March 7, 1994.

similar, and yet, unforeseen dilemmas encountered in these two distinct socioeducational research contexts are discussed in terms of institutional, methodological, and ethical issues, along with the compromises and insights that they engendered. We explore the underpinnings of some of these issues and the notion that in school-based research of the type undertaken here, modifications in research agendas may be inevitable. Furthermore, we claim that as more qualitative research is undertaken in classrooms with limited English-proficient students during times of rapid social change, many of our assumptions about the need to maintain the integrity of predetermined, static research designs and methods, perspectives derived from experimental, quantitative research paradigms, must be critically examined.

CHANGING CONTEXTS AND RESEARCH AGENDAS

The past few years have witnessed some significant changes in the scope of classroom research involving second language (L2) learners and also in methodological approaches to research (e.g., Johnson, 1992). In this section we deal with each of these in turn.

Changes in Scope

Exciting new developments are taking place in the areas of cognition and learning in L2 classroom contexts in terms of implicit learning, input processing, and the role of instructional interventions on acquisition (cf. Lightbown, Spada, & White, 1993), and in studies of cognitive apprenticeship through academic or real-world tasks (Lave, 1988; Lave & Wenger, 1991; Rogoff, 1990; Swain, 1995). Furthermore, interesting new directions in ethnography and ESL are being pursued (cf. Bailey & Nunan, in press; Davis, 1995; Duff, 1995; Johnson, 1992; Lazaraton, 1995; van Lier, 1988; Watson-Gegeo, 1988; Willett, 1995), and action research is being embraced as an alternative to traditional approaches in classroom research (Crookes, 1993; Nunan, 1990; Wells

& Chang-Wells, 1992). Until relatively recently, however, re-search on L2 learners and teachers has primarily taken place in either experimental classroomlike laboratory settings or in second or foreign language classrooms, as opposed to content classrooms or other contexts of learning such as homes, playgrounds, or vocational settings.

According to one extensive literature review (Chaudron, 1988), the focus of L2 studies carried out in the 1970s and 1980s tended to be single issues or domains of inquiry fall-ing under one of three general headings listed and illus-trated below:

1. *Teacher talk*: examining the amount and type of teacher talk, questions teachers ask, speech modifi-cations they make, and feedback they provide stu-dents.
2. *Learners' individual and group behaviors*: examining developmental aspects of learners' language, personal learning styles and strategies, and the effects of dif-ferent topics and task types on learners' language.
3. *Student–teacher interaction*: examining the effect of interactional modifications on learners' ability to com-prehend and acquire the target language.

Much L2 classroom research since the 1980's has, then, examined language use (input, interaction, and output) in settings with relatively little attention paid to the nonlinguistic context or the content of discussions. Issues concerning the immediate linguistic environment and be-havior of subjects have thus been foregrounded, and broader socioeducational environments backgrounded along with issues of culture, community, and politics (local, regional, national, and international), and learner perspectives on research (see Johnson, 1992). Not coincidentally, this body of now mainstream research reflects the dominant theories of the day which, in our field, tend to draw heavily upon models, methodologies, and questions favored in linguis-tics, psychology, and related fields. Researchers taking an interactionist stance naturally also recognize the importance of environmental factors, such as the social and linguistic roles played by caregivers, teachers, siblings, and peers in providing language input (Larsen-Freeman & Long, 1991). However, we see the potential for new directions in classroom research and for a more critical examination of what constitutes context in research (cf. Breen, 1985; Duranti & Goodwin, 1992).

The claim that our studies of language and other aspects of learning, and ultimately theory construction as well, tend to take for granted and not explicitly acknowledge the broader social context in which input and interaction are generated has been advanced for some time (Hatch & Hawkins, 1987; Lantolf & Appel, 1994), and further developed by scholars with a critical theoretical outlook, such as Kramsch (1993) and Pennycook (1990). These authors may represent the minority, however. Second language studies still continue to examine fine-tuned linguistic measures of input, output, and meaning negotiation for students enrolled in language classes, using reasonably well controlled, (frequently) small-scale data collection procedures and quantifiable measures putatively linked to successful L2 acquisition (e.g., Gass & Varonis, 1994; Loschky, 1994).

This research has been very valuable in the development of understandings about L2 development and classroom discourse, and it will no doubt continue to play an important role in our field. Furthermore, language classrooms remain an essential site for the examination and testing of research, theory, and practice in applied linguistics. However, in addition to this ongoing work, we believe it is now timely for the research agenda to be expanded in response to the range of challenges surfacing in schools and other multilingual institutions today, which applied linguists are increasingly being called upon to deal with (Pennycook, 1990). One impetus for this call is the mushrooming population of L2 learners worldwide, and particularly children, who are receiving their education through English, their L2. Some 8,000,000 children in the United States alone are not learning their L2 in language classrooms, but rather in mainstream content classrooms (Waggoner, 1992, cited in Crandall, 1993, p. 127). Similar trends can be found both in large urban centers and in isolated indigenous communities in Canada as well. The study of these children's language socialization in regular classrooms necessarily opens up and redirects the aims and issues addressed in classroom research and, indeed, shifts the venue from language classrooms to content classrooms, and the focus from language in a generic sense to language associated with specific content or vocational areas. In addition, an acknowledgement of the relevance and importance of examining cultural discontinuities in children's home and school language activities (e.g., with respect to literacy) or between school programs and societal or work expectations for adults takes us well beyond the realm of linguistic dimensions of classroom language use alone (see Ogbu, 1982).

Simply transferring existing research agendas to new contexts is unwise, however, because the issues of interest to stakeholders often extend well beyond the development of discrete, sentence-level linguistic structures to studies of a more holistic and often interpretive or transformative nature. Language forms and functions may need to be examined in terms of broader educational issues, such as assessment, curriculum, multiculturalism, socioeconomic reproduction, and academic discourses. Added to these are a host of other affective and interpersonal variables related to the particular populations that are being served and studied. Questions now being asked include, for example: What factors affect or are related to the language that people use and learn and, hence, their academic (or vocational) success and future opportunities? And, conversely, what impact do the learners and their language use and needs have on the contexts in which they find themselves?

PARADIGM SHIFTS: SOME PROBLEMATICS OF ADOPTING QUALITATIVE METHODOLOGIES TO ADDRESS BROADER QUESTIONS

Positivism and Naturalism: Oil and Water?

Although the shift in both scope and research questions referred to above suggests the use of a wider range of research methods and approaches, and in particular, various qualitative, field-based ones, the past few years have seen less of an actual change in the implementation of these methodologies than in the recognition of their importance. For example, L2 classroom researchers (Larsen-Freeman & Long, 1991; Ulichny, 1989; van Lier, 1988) and authors of texts on ESL research methods (Hatch & Lazaraton, 1991; Nunan, 1992; Seliger & Shohamy, 1989) have argued for more rigorous, multimethod forms of analysis and/or broader, longitudinal, sociocontextually based research (Fisher, 1990; Miles & Huberman, 1984; Patton, 1988; Reichardt & Cook, 1979). Yet, reviews of L2 classroom research (e.g., Mitchell, 1985) continue to reveal a preference or bias toward quantitative, process–product investigations of classroom behaviors, even when more inductive approaches have been included. At the same time, much current work in other areas of the humanities and social sciences, influenced by phenomenological ideologies, favors critical, interpretive, layered analyses of human behaviors and interactions, viewing these as highly complex and contingent and not easily given to quantitative measurement or categorical reduction. In addition, increasingly there is a call for an explicit acknowledgement of the researcher's own role in the research enterprise and how this bears upon the collection of data and the interpretation of results (Gal, 1989; Lather, 1991).

Calls for more rigor and for recognition of the legitimacy of a range of approaches in our research are warranted and promise rich data for analysis, sometimes in previously unexplored domains. For that reason, we have attempted to include both qualitative and quantitative dimensions in our own work. However, our attempts to do so have occasionally brought us face to face with issues long debated by methodologists about the potential incompatibilities or problematics of trying to simultaneously and eclectically embrace epistemological perspectives which, in their idealized forms, are often construed as mutually exclusive; the quantitative paradigm conceives of reality as objective, divisible into measurable, discrete parts, with closed, convergent, linear systems, whereas the qualitative paradigm recognizes multiple realities which must be viewed holistically, with open, divergent, circular–complex systems undergoing constant refinement and adaptation (Guba & Lincoln, 1988; Miles & Huberman, 1988; Patton, 1988). Sometimes trying to achieve an ecumenical blend (a term from Miles & Huberman, 1984) is, in both theory and practice, like trying to combine oil and water, to use a metaphor from Guba and Lincoln (1988). Probably a greater obstacle than either managing research using both paradigms or attempting to expand qualitative ones is that "qualitative methods are still the poor relative of quantitative approaches" (Patton, 1988, p. 133). Indeed, this may account for the paucity of larger multimethod, longitudinal, socioculturally grounded classroom research, despite some headway being made in that direction. Other reasons may derive from the nature of funding competitions, the cost of implementing a comprehensive broad-based project, and constraints on publication, given that most journals still appear to favor short articles presenting original quantitative studies, although that too may be changing as a survey of recent issues of the *TESOL Quarterly* reveals, for example (e.g., Davis & Lazaraton, 1995).

The Reporting of Problematics

One of the tangible results of the sometimes uneasy marriage of the two approaches is that there remains across both quantitative and qualitative research an overreliance on conventional positivistic criteria, concepts, and assumptions. This may yield clear, concise research reports which, one gets the impression, underreport some of the problems, divergent interpretations, and limitations of the classroom research in their particular settings. In the move toward more complex, wider-ranging, and long-term research programs in a variety of unique contexts, this should be addressed.[2] However, in the reporting of these same issues, it is clear that the scientific academic discourse to which we

---

[2]A few years ago, a number of humorous, yet instructive, anecdotal reports of the hazards and pitfalls of research projects conducted by applied linguists were compiled by Swain and Cumming (1989), although in the original authors' published accounts of these same studies it is un-

have become accustomed may also require reanalysis and modification (Lather, 1991).

In literature pertaining to L2 program evaluation research (cf. Beretta, 1992; Coleman, 1992), authors are sometimes explicit in providing reports of the ongoing modifications in the objectives and means of enacting evaluations, including the need to sometimes "move the goalposts" (Coleman, 1992) for various unforeseen practical reasons. Beretta (1992) provided the following perspective:

> Evaluation reports that give the impression of a smooth, professional operation that went off without a hitch are far from the mark. Current thinking in evaluation would deny the validity of such impressions. Discussion with other evaluators, my own experience, and established perspectives in the evaluation literature (e.g., Cronbach et al., 1980) suggest that a more realistic picture would present a messy, chaotic series of compromises, where classic research designs disintegrate, where vain hopes of contributing to certain kinds of learning theory are soon dispelled, and where all that lies between the pragmatic evaluator and scholarly perdition is a sense of disciplined inquiry, whether it relates to quasi-experimental research, to a host of naturalistic approaches, or to policy analysis. (p. 250)

As Alderson and Beretta (1992) remarked, "hindsight is not only the most exact science; it is also the discipline best able to give the impression of order, rationality, and careful planning" (p. 272). The misleading and idealistic assump-

---

likely that the researchers explicitly reflected upon the theoretical or ideological significance of the apparent lapses in their expertise. For example, Swain and Cumming noted that these lapses or glitches often resulted from "the artificial imposition of scientific methods onto human behaviour" or from "children's spontaneous actions, from administrative confusions, or from differing cross-cultural expectations" (p. 89). Interestingly, many of what were considered to be aberrations in the studies actually derived from subjects' perceptions of the research activity and its goals (cf. Coughlan & Duff, 1994); their surprise at being asked questions with obvious answers or with little perceived communicative value (Swain & Cumming, 1989, pp. 98-99) for the sake of carefully controlled hypotheticodeductive inquiry.

tion is that had there been better communication and planning prior to the onset of the research, "[t]here would be no mystery, no surprises" (Beretta, 1992, p. 264). Our experience reveals the contrary: Mysteries and surprises are inevitable when researchers attempt to carry out long-term projects in social settings with a multiplicity of individuals, agendas, and institutions and an inquiry process with elements of emergent design (Guba & Lincoln, 1988). Of course, the utility and wisdom of planning well and opening up clear lines of communication with participants is undeniable; but change is part and parcel of every socially contextualized research enterprise, and particularly so in schools in urban centers today with shifting demographic patterns and priorities. Thus, part of our socialization as educational researchers entails learning to come to terms with those mysteries and surprises, to somehow find a place for them in our many-layered texts and to consider what has given rise to them and what theoretical significance they might have. Patton (1988) claimed that researchers don't report fully enough about their methodology; the "crucial underpinnings of analysis remain mostly implicit, explained only allusively" (p. 127). The nature of research and accountability in reporting must therefore be examined because this phenomenon goes well beyond negligence among researchers.

Because of space, oversight, or caution, then, the elimination of discussions of the problematics and compromises (to use words which again cast in negative terms this natural process) encountered in a particular project reduces contextual information that is essential to fully understand the project, to interpret the results, to draw pedagogical implications, and to propose interesting directions for relevant research in other domains, not to mention those needed to undertake studies of a similar nature in another setting. It is with this intent that this chapter seeks to report on some of the complexities of classroom research that each of us has grappled with in our respective settings in Canada and Hungary. In the following section, therefore, we present in some detail the contexts of our research and then move from the discussions of the unique aspects of our respective experiences to more general issues related to classroom research.

RESEARCH SITES

Table 1.1 provides an outline of the sites, goals, and methods for the two research projects and changes that occurred
in these over time. It also highlights the nature of the research teams and the funding for each, which were important factors in determining the scope and nature of data
collection and analysis. In the sections that follow, examples
are generally provided for one or the other context, with the
understanding that the examples represent issues in both
contexts to a certain degree.

The Canadian Study

In the Canadian context, the research has spanned 7 years
and was undertaken in two phases. Phase one, from 1987
to 1991, initially involved the establishment of teams of
teachers in 8 elementary and 4 secondary schools in the
Vancouver school districts. Each team consisted of both ESL
and content teachers. These teachers participated in a series of related in-service sessions on the following topics;
Mohan's (1986) theoretical framework for integrating language and content instruction; relationships among knowledge structures, discourse, and graphics (in that framework);
the representation of knowledge structures in discourse and
graphic forms; and the uses of graphics by teachers and
students. Workshops were also given on cooperative learning activities for student and teacher collaboration. In addition, the sessions assisted the teachers in developing the-
matic units and instructional strategies for ESL students
in both ESL and content classrooms. The process was continued with other teachers within the initial project schools
and extended to a large number of new schools in subsequent years. The targeted subject areas other than the ESL
classrooms were science, social studies, and computer studies.

Originally the project proposal had a process–product
design with formative and summative evaluation components. However, action research emerged as a complemen-
tary approach (Carr & Kemmis, 1986) very early in the implementation, forged by the growing collaboration of the two
local principal researchers, Early and Mohan, and the vari-

TABLE 1.1
Research Sites

	Hungary	*Canada*
Sites	3 experimental dual- language secondary schools in different cities (control school dropped)	12 schools initially; 8 elementary, 4 secondary
Time frame	1989-1992 Follow-up visit 1993	1987-1990 2nd Project 1990-present
Original goals	Formative & summative evaluation; monitor progress in EFL, content areas, attitudes/motivation and make recommendations; feedback to schools, Hungarian Ministry of Education, pedagogical research institutes, UCLA	Formative & summative evaluation; implement and monitor progress in using an integrated approach to teaching language and content; feedback to schools, district and BC Ministry of Education
Methods	Language testing, questionnaires, essays, interviews, classroom observations	Analysis of student records, classroom discourse, essays, questionnaires, interviews, observations
Revised goals	Classroom research/ethnography of communication in Hungarian-medium history classrooms focusing on language (re)socialization in that context and through that content	Action research in classrooms (mostly science, social and computer studies) focusing on language socialization in that context and through that content
Methods	Interviews, essays, video taped lessons by 8 teachers, microanalysis of one event	Case studies, interviews, observations, experiments, discourse analysis
Team	One nonlocal researcher with some local teacher/ student support	Two local researchers plus team of teacher–researchers and graduate students
Funding	USIA, Hungarian Ministry (1989-1991; small grants) Spencer Foundation (1992)	BC Ministry of Education, Vancouver School Board (1987-1989), SSHRC ('91-pres)

ous stakeholder groups with whom they were working. The study thus also benefited from the participation of both graduate students and teacher–researchers. Quantitative and qualitative research methods were employed, involving measures of the effects of experimental instructional treatment types on students' performance, questionnaires, interviews, analysis of student discourse, case studies of teachers and students, and so on.

The second phase, from 1991 to the present, is funded by the Social Sciences and Humanities Research Council of Canada (SSHRC) and is conducted in one elementary and one secondary school in Vancouver. The research program consists of qualitative and quantitative studies of teaching in which teachers and their ESL students are being studied while they plan, implement, and assess integrated language and content instruction in their science and social studies classes. In addition, quantitative quasiexperimental studies of learning are being conducted to examine the effects of different types of tasks on ESL students' comprehension of oral and written expository discourse in social studies and science.

This research has been conducted in a sociopolitical and educational context which has been less stable than one might assume for a west coast Canadian province. This can be attributed, at least in part, to a study by the Royal Commission on Education conducted just prior to the project years (Sullivan, 1988), which resulted in the implementation of a series of processes to radically change the primary, intermediate, and graduation programs. Curricula were consequently subjected to ongoing revisions of a substantial and far-reaching nature; methods of instruction, assessment, evaluation, and reporting on student performance were also undergoing reform. An additional and very important factor was that the Vancouver school district saw a dramatic and rapid increase in the ESL population, particularly at the high school level. Changes were observed in the ethnic composition, literacy, and educational backgrounds of the new student body, based on teachers' past experiences working with ESL children (e.g., a 94% increase in Spanish children since 1982, new Somali and Khmer populations, and growing populations of Cantonese, Mandarin, Vietnamese, Korean, and Punjabi speaking students (H. Hooper, personal communication, Oct. 1, 1994; Galloway, Marshall, Morgan, Muir, & Rooney, 1994). As a result, in the Vancouver school system, ESL students now comprise more than half the students in mainstream programs.

The Hungarian Study

In the Hungarian context, an experimental approach to L2 instruction was introduced by the Ministry of Education in the mid-to late-1980s, at a critical juncture in Eastern European politics when proficiency in Western European languages became an educational priority. Late-immersion (dual-language) programs of two types were thus established in a number of academic secondary schools across the country. Although several different foreign languages were involved, English was one of the most popular. The research was designed to provide the first formative and summative evaluation of several content-based L2 programs. The main focus of the study was initially an investigation of the development of EFL skills in that context, as well as an examination of students' attitudes and motivation to study in these experimental programs; student performance in the content areas was also informally examined. Thus, the research was originally envisioned in 1989 as a typical process–product study by one primary researcher under the auspices of the Language Resource Program at the University of California, Los Angeles (Duff, 1991). The Hungarian Ministry of Education and its subsidiary pedagogical institutes also provided support for the research.

Because of both a combination of constraints on formal testing of L2 and content, and the monumental changes taking place outside the schools, the study took on an added dimension in 1991; an in-depth examination of the educational discourse within 3 dual-language schools, and especially the discourse of local assessment practices. This shift in focus was neither predetermined nor accidental, however. It simply reflected the sociopolitical and educational reforms put into place between 1985 and 1989, in particular, and a shift in what was considered most intriguing at the time. To pursue the first set of research objectives without examining the interface of both macro and microcontexts for language learning and use would have been myopic and would have created difficulties in the interpretation of some of the quantitative findings. Using constitutive ethnographic methodology, the researcher went on to explore the evolution of a genre of assessment used in the experimental programs, and in history lessons, in particular, and how participants' roles, expectations, and linguistic behaviors were in the process of changing in response to, and as part of, sociopolitical transformation (Duff, 1993, 1995). The study was formally discontinued after 1992, aside from brief follow-up visits and long distance communication, for several reasons such as the practical difficulties of conducting research on another continent; the researcher's relocation within North America; changes in funding; and a perception of the increasingly political (and politicized) nature of the research enterprise itself, in light of the sometimes competing demands and yet dwindling resources of local institutes, the Ministry, universities, and schools.

CONSIDERATIONS IN THE PROBLEMATICS OF CLASSROOM RESEARCH

In the following sections, we present in more general terms (and thus deliberately employ the present tense) a range of issues which surfaced in the course of the Hungarian and Canadian studies. We intentionally distance ourselves from precise details of one or the other context in order to demonstrate more common (if not universal) aspects of school-based research, regardless of sociopolitical setting, and also to preserve good working relations within those settings. However, we hasten to point out that the discussion of institutional, methodological, and ethical dimensions of classroom research derive from two very specific sets of experiences.

Institutional (Sociopolitical) Considerations

When researchers undertake studies in school settings, multiple stakeholders are usually involved: government funding agencies, ministries of education, pedagogical institutes, school district officials, school administrators, teachers' professional associations, and so on. Each of these generally brings its own agenda to a large-scale project. When researchers are negotiating access to sites, conflicting agendas become evident over such issues as the number and choice of the sites. And yet, some may not be as principally focused on the research agenda as the researchers. For example, local officials may view an innovation as an opportunity for in-service work and may want it to be more widespread than the researchers believe is manageable; likewise, teachers' associations may want resources attached to a project spread more equitably across a number of schools rather than being focused on one or two inequitably resource-rich sites.

Site selection can therefore be a contentious issue. Researchers may wish to work in schools known for their positive characteristics (good climate, low student/teacher turnover, especially highly qualified staff, etc.), whereas district officials or administrators may view a project as a potential means of turning around a school with a less positive reputation. The use and safeguarding of research funds can also be an area of potential conflict of interest, particularly when projects are jointly funded to collaborating districts and universities, both with signing authority. Even when one has recourse to an original proposal, interpretations can differ and circumstances can change over time, necessitating the renegotiation of how and where funding will be applied. In addition, multiple stakeholders can call into question issues relating to ownership of materials, including data, reports, texts, and measurements.

Institutions also change over time. In the two geographical contexts outlined above, rapid changes of a fairly dramatic nature occurred for the duration of the projects. Although these may seem like extreme examples of instability and change, they are perhaps not so unusual in the modern world in which we live. School districts and schools are dynamic contexts continually undergoing some degree of curricular revision and continually attempting to improve and be responsive to larger societal changes. The implementation of innovations, of course, means that district and school sites are in constant flux.

Some of the ways in which change has had an observable impact on our own research programs follow (see Table 1.2). Ministries of Education and school districts commonly undergo internal restructuring in response to changes in national, provincial/state, or local government program policies, and colleagues who have been involved in formulating research agendas can be reassigned to new positions. New officials are then assigned to be research collaborators. These tend to be highly professional individuals, who naturally wish to influence and, in some measure, contribute to the research agenda. However, it generally requires time and negotiation to bring about change of this interpersonal nature smoothly. Turnover in colleagues at other levels is also likely to occur. Administrators are assigned to new schools, teachers take leaves (maternity, educational, etc.), or move to new schools and districts. Key project teachers frequently assume new leadership roles within school, university, and district offices. In times of downsizing and restructuring, layoffs, resignations, and reassignments also occur. Indeed, teacher turnover provides a series of challenges to the continuity and design of original project plans.

Likewise, in particular contexts (e.g., in large North American, Australian, and Western European cities, but less so in Hungary in the early 1990s), the student population is rapidly changing. This again can create considerable turmoil for research subjects. For example, in their settlement process, incoming students move to new places of residence frequently when they first arrive in a district and they must then move to new schools in their neighborhood. They find themselves in constantly changing timetables as schools try to accommodate them. Among other things, this migration of students makes continuity difficult to achieve among sample groups. Furthermore, and again in the Canadian context, whole districts can experience dramatic demographic shifts in the student population. The implementation of new curricula and subsequent changes in methods of instruction and in the materials and resources used, together with related in-service programs offered to support such changes, can seriously impinge upon the time teachers and students have to spend with researchers. Finally, dilemmas and pressures are encountered by researchers

TABLE 1.2
Institutional (Sociopolitical) Considerations

---

1. *Sociopolitical context*
2. *Multiple stakeholders*—influencing the following:
   a. site selection (number & choice of sites)
   b. teacher/classroom selection (number, choice, & range)
   c. research funds (availability, safeguarding, & use)
   d. communication within and across stakeholder groups
   e. ownership of materials (data, reports, etc.)
3. *Prevailing attitudes to educational research*
4. *Time frames*
5. *Possible changes encountered:*
   a. funding sources
   b. Ministry reorganization
   c. local reorganization
   d. staff and officials at all levels; relationships among participants
   e. students—demographics, attrition
   f. schools—decreasing time for teachers and students to spend with researchers
   g. researchers' role(s) in schools—new demands related to many of the above issues

---

who themselves may simultaneously be playing different social roles; the tension is based on the desire to be supportive of colleagues and students at all levels, yet to not jeopardize the success of the research program.

Another institutional challenge is posed by communication within and across stakeholder groups. Practical problems may be mitigated by access to technology for communication (e.g., phones, faxes, electronic mail—originally unavailable or difficult to access in Hungary), by the establishment of newsletters to disseminate ongoing developments, and by regular meetings with optimal numbers of participants. Unreasonable time frames need to be negotiated and renegotiated in keeping with our growing understanding of the length of time it takes to establish trusting, productive working relations and to effect any kind of measurable change. Moreover, the belief some participants have that educational research will ultimately have little impact on teachers' and students' daily lives and classroom practices needs to be examined and worked through.

All of these areas demand critical reflection as well as strategic planning on the part of researchers, for whom

published discussions of similar issues, dilemmas, and research processes may be very instructive.

Methodological Considerations

Overlapping with the institutional concerns presented in
the previous section are those relating to research methods, especially the design and implementation of proposed
projects (see Table 1.3). As was mentioned in the discussion of paradigm shifts, despite prescriptions and assur-
ances to the contrary (e.g., Reichardt & Cook, 1979), both
our studies found it challenging to attempt to strike a meaningful balance between quantitative and qualitative approaches to studying classroom phenomena and to representing fairly both emic (insider) and etic (outsider) perspectives in ethnographic work. As the two studies progressed, their orientation evolved and became increasingly
adaptive, interpretive, and inductive. In the Canadian study,
collaborative action research was introduced as one facet
of this endeavor. Input and responsiveness from teachers
and other participants is an essential part of action research,
as questions and contingencies arise; consequently, design
features change with the introduction of new curricular innovations and the reappraisal of research and instructional
goals. In the following paragraphs, we present in general
terms some of the methodological decisions we grappled
with.

Dozens of methodological issues are encountered on an
ongoing basis in comprehensive classroom research of this
nature. The time frame for the study, when to begin and
end it, must be carefully considered; but this is also linked
to sources of funding, which are often unpredictable. After
months or even years of applying, they may only be announced and awarded at the commencement of the academic year for which funding was requested and granted.

The selection and number of research sites is also critical. A multisite design, which both of the present studies
opted for, offers both advantages and disadvantages. On
the one hand, it provides a range of situations and a wider
pool of participants and backgrounds than a single case
would normally yield. On the other hand, the researcher's

TABLE 1.3
Methodological Considerations

Approach
- Demands of attempting to embrace both quantitative and qualitative approaches
- Challenges posed by seeking balance in both emic and etic perspectives; for example, in coding, analysis, and interpretation of results
- Need to come to terms with quickly changing sociopolitical context both inside and outside schools with apparent effects on observed behaviors

Design
- Time frame for study; when to begin and end
- Unanticipated changes in curriculum
- Selection/composition of experimental versus control groups
- Tension between breadth versus depth in surveying sites
- Need to reconstitute (or add, delete) groups
- Implementation of experimental treatment with controls
- Selection of test instruments
- Need for more relevant instrument development (e.g., content-area tests) beyond the scope of researchers' expertise and project goals
- Decisions concerning technology; for example, audio versus video recording

Participants
- Students' reactions to innovations and test instruments—for example, resistance
- Attrition or changing roles among participants

---

inability to maintain a presence at any one site over a long period of time has drawbacks, restricting the continuity, the depth of understanding, and the credibility and trust that come from being closely connected with one site, with one group of people, and with changing local circumstances. Conducting the research from afar or by proxy also involves tradeoffs. Over time, groups are reconstituted, added, or deleted from the original design as it becomes clearer that the researchers' goals and the contributions of particular groups to the attainment of those goals diverge.

In studies of an experimental nature, the composition of control and experimental groups is an important consideration but one that is not easy to secure in most educational settings. Typically, constraints exist with respect to the random assignment of subjects to groups and the delivery of varying treatments (or conditions) to them. Furthermore, even when groups have been carefully composed, teachers may not deliver the treatment type intended for their group. They may instead embrace a more eclectic approach to teaching than the one assigned or introduce elements of the experimental treatment to control groups with the belief that the experimental, often innovative treatment is indeed superior to the nontreatment condition and that it would therefore be unethical to knowingly withhold it.

The previous section has already highlighted the pervasiveness of turnover among students, teachers, and officials in urban areas with high levels of professional and personal mobility in times of heavy immigration and socioeconomic restructuring. This has ramifications for the design and outcomes of our studies. In addition to attrition, students in school-based studies (particularly at the secondary level) are sometimes simply uncooperative, resisting treatments or not taking seriously the tests or innovations which they feel have no direct bearing upon their school grades, or which are unfamiliar or uninteresting in light of the more pressing sociopolitical, academic, and personal concerns competing for their attention. And when students learn of dismissals or resignations among their teachers, they may naturally feel less committed to planned testing sessions. All of these realities must be dealt with by researchers on a day-by-day, case-by-case basis, and all of them underscore the importance of understanding local contexts well when conducting research there.

Another methodological consideration has to do with the availability and use of technology, such as audio versus video recording. Although this might seem to be a purely practical or logistical matter, it also reflects underlying theoretical assumptions about the nature of the object of enquiry, just as the means of representing data in transcripts has ideological as well as methodological bases (Ochs, 1979). The financial consequences of these decisions are relevant not only to the purchasing of equipment but also the hiring of research assistants to collect, transcribe, and analyze the data, which may include languages other than English.

Where test instruments are required by the design, selection issues may prove very demanding. For example, are locally produced (criterion referenced) instruments necessary and, if so, who will prepare and pilot test them? In tests of language in the content areas, the dilemma may be whether to seek the expertise and collaboration of content specialists (e.g., physicists and historians) and not just applied linguists. This concern is particularly acute in immersion or mainstream classroom studies but it is often a far more complex undertaking than researchers might have envisioned, and only realized when other test items or instruments fail. Students' reactions to or perceptions of innovations and tests, which may help account for their performance, can be ascertained through introspective or retrospective interviews in order to validate procedures and also to provide insider perspectives on the procedures, which facilitates the interpretation of results. Hence, this too needs to be anticipated when designing studies.

Ethical Considerations

Professional organizations and institutional review boards attempt to establish regulations to ensure that human research subjects are treated ethically. These principles and guidelines are undoubtedly helpful to researchers, but they may be neither self-evident nor absolute. Thus, interpretations or judgments often reside with the individual researcher or team. Based upon our experience, ethical issues or concerns may arise in several areas (see Table 1.4; see also LeCompte & Preissle, 1993, chapter 4).

The first of these is related to privacy and confidentiality. Although it is common practice to change the names of research subjects, this in itself does not guarantee subject anonymity. In reports of school-based research, prominent individuals or focal subjects tend to be more vulnerable than others. For example, although there are many teachers at a given school, there is usually just one principal and maybe only one ESL teacher. Similarly, in case studies of students, some may be identified as more or less successful or capable. These individuals are, thus, more prone to recognition by others. In addition, the use of quotation, which gives voice to the participants, can at the same time serve to mark individuals, if not to a general audience, then to other members in the research setting, either by virtue of their known position on a topic or by their voice quality.

In a more subtle vein, issues of privacy can also be called into question when researchers' notions of personal boundaries differ from those of the research subjects. In these circumstances, we run the risk of transgressing subjects' sense of propriety by being overly intrusive. This, in turn, can lead to yet another ethical concern: the risk of unwittingly causing possible harm to the subjects. In the first instance, the visibility of the subjects can pose potential future ramifications for them. For example, where school officials (e.g., certain principals and vice principals) and their favorite innovations are viewed with disdain by teachers and students, the disclosure of these sentiments could have implications for future promotions or contract renewals. Untenured teachers may be particularly at risk. In the second instance, intrusiveness may also be harmful when subjects, either from feelings of powerlessness or confusion about obligations to the researcher, reveal more than they may wish and later suffer from a range of negative emotions as a result of their misgivings. Admittedly, research in the field of applied or educational linguistics is fraught with fewer potential risks than many other types of work; nonetheless, we found ourselves deliberating about some

TABLE 1.4
Ethical Considerations

Privacy and confidentiality
- Protection of focal individuals or people whose views/voice are recognizable
- Awareness of relative intrusiveness of research

Security
- Future ramifications of identification of dissenting individuals
- Consequences of researcher intrusiveness

Researcher integrity
- Fairness to all stakeholders

Methodology
- Denial of experimental/innovative treatments to control groups in the face of dissent

of these very issues during our studies. Another quandary has been how to ensure that we are contextualizing the findings appropriately and fairly, according to the source's intended meanings.

Other matters that raise ethical questions and moral dilemmas for researchers relate to matters of (inter)personal integrity on the part of researchers, for example, how to handle conflicts that arise between the various stakeholder groups so as to maintain cooperation with members of various groups and not alienate members of others. Similarly, how and to which audience to report cross-group conflicts and differing perspectives on issues can also test researchers' credibility, fairness, and judgment. Additional considerations, including decisions about enforcing control treatments in the face of apparently more successful experimental treatments (referred to in the previous section), are listed in Table 1.4.

IMPLICATIONS OF PROBLEMATICS:
JUDGED BY WHAT STANDARDS?

In discussions of our respective research projects, we have found remarkable similarities in the types of unforeseen institutional, methodological, and ethical issues we have encountered. Each decision had consequences for the research as well as for our relationships with those that we were working with in the schools. Control groups were deleted, schools with high rates of attrition were eliminated, and schools with particularly acute problems of another nature were not targeted for research in the manner intended. Compromises were (somewhat reluctantly) reached about uninvited teacher or student interventions in nontreatment classrooms or during test sessions. Test instruments were dropped, modified, or redesigned. The results that seemed irregular (suggesting, for example, cheating or apathy on tests) were analyzed separately or were dropped. A good deal of energy was expended to simply preserve working channels of communication with administrators and teachers in the face of higher than expected turnover. Finally, original research objectives which no longer seemed appropriate, useful, or feasible were modified, usually resulting in more comprehensive, qualitative analyses of classroom activities and in the triangulation of a wider range of ethnographic data.

To delve into the details of compromises such as these would occupy more space than we have here. However, one issue not yet addressed is the following: Despite, or perhaps in view of, the problematics outlined above, what can be construed as success in school- based classroom research projects? How can ongoing research of this nature be justified to stakeholders, grant-providers, and the academy, given the kinds of inevitable adjustments that arise and that potentially threaten the integrity (to use traditional terminology) of the projects as they were conceived? Regardless of the findings generated by the research, how can participants benefit from the research enterprise itself and become more responsive and involved in the process? We do not pretend to have answers to these questions ourselves and are, rather, still in a process of evaluating, synthesizing, and learning from our own experiences. However, Guba and Lincoln (1989) have suggested three types of criteria for judging relative success, based on their work in project evaluation.

The first set is intended to parallel the conventional criteria of internal validity, external validity, reliability, and objectivity, long-established standards in the framework of logical positivism. The authors refer to these criteria collectively as indices of trustworthiness. They include credibility and transferability, which are achieved through prolonged engagement, persistent observation, reflection, and "thick description" (Geertz, 1973), for example, descriptors related to the reporter's objectivity and care in documenting the process (see Hopkins, 1989). Second, Guba and Lincoln (1989) utilized the hermeneutic process itself as its own quality control. This involves feedback to participants for verification, clarity, and explanation of the data. The third category relates to the authenticity of the project and results, with considerations of fairness (e.g., vis-à-vis stakeholders, negotiations, etc.), ontological authenticity or the improvement or maturation of participants' perceptions and awareness of their experiences, and then what they call educative, catalytic, and tactical authenticity. This latter set refers to the insights that are gained by participants, and the extent to which these insights stimulate further action, especially by participants and in their best interests.

In summary, we have presented here a number of criteria by which researchers might evaluate their work. Whereas our ongoing academic ventures are often fueled and validated by such measures as renewed support from grant-giving agencies and enthusiasm on the part of our research communities, heightened researcher awareness and insights must derive from considerations of a more philosophical and critical nature as well (LeCompte & Preissle, 1993).

CONCLUSION

In this final section, we consider some of the factors that we have learned are invaluable in longterm classroom research. First, from scholars in qualitative research, we have learned the value of negotiating site entry, establishing with stakeholder groups preconditions to conducting the research (Erickson, 1986), and regularly renegotiating these so as to ensure maximum control and consensus over the studies and an increased understanding of what we would like to do and what others would have us do. Discussing in advance issues related to access to data, confidentiality, and so on, is one aspect of this. In his book on the politics and ethics of evaluation, Adelman (1984) recommended that rolling contracts be drafted and redrafted among relevant parties throughout a project (term-by-term or year-by-year), in response to changes, local circumstances and contingencies, and revised research objectives. Further, he noted how reports can be disseminated (e.g., from the top down or among closest colleagues) in a limited way to invite feedback and comment prior to wider distribution. In short, our original research designs must be viewed as templates as opposed to blueprints, which must be fleshed out on a continuing basis.

Second, we have learned that the quantitative–qualitative research distinction and calls for a balance between the two are not as uncomplicated as one might expect. Reflecting on Reichardt and Cook's (1979) suggestion some time ago that researchers go beyond an untenable division of the two (claiming to embrace one or the other), trying to embrace both is not altogether straightforward either. That is because the dominant paradigm remains the quantitative one, which in effect dwarfs and discourages attempts to undertake more truly qualitative studies. We would, therefore, like to see more well-conceived qualitative work which helps to reverse this trend and the underlying belief that quantitative investigations are not only superior but also represent the culmination of scientific enquiry.

Third, along with the other changes, we sense the need to begin to think in different ways from those we have become accustomed to, with increasing self-awareness and critical insight, as both researchers and scholars. We are social actors and agents in our research activities, and with this agency comes tremendous power, responsibility, experience, and learning. As our professional socialization thus continues, we recognize the need for continuing language resocialization, as well, so we can report upon our research clearly and in a spirit that both reflects our ontological assumptions, and disseminates our findings appropriately as well.

Finally, we believe that the dismissal or downplaying of problematics such as we have addressed here constitutes a disservice to other researchers, and particularly those with less experience. Because relatively few long-term ethnographic, qualitative studies of classroom language use have been undertaken in our field, and because change and complexity appear to be the order of the day in social institutions, an understanding of the compromises or decisions others have had to reach can be instructive for colleagues in similar situations. We thus encourage more open discussion of research problematics, methodology, and underlying philosophical biases that may otherwise impede productive classroom research.

POSTSCRIPT: THE DIALECTICS OF REFLECTION IN CLASSROOM RESEARCH

Related to the call for greater researcher reflectiveness, we would like to close with a few remarks about the language with which we report our classroom research, processes, outcomes, and decisions. In the writing of this chapter, for example, we caught ourselves unconsciously producing a seemingly endless list of terms such as problem, problematics (as in the title), concerns, difficulties, dilemmas, threats to integrity, and so on. Increasingly, we became aware of the negative values we were ascribing to various aspects of our research and also recognized the possible root source of these harsh judgments, in positivism. On the one hand, we were seemingly applauding research embracing emergent designs, multiple realities, and so on; yet, on the other hand, we were reporting our ever-changing situations in terms that suggested failure in conception, execution, and termination, according to logicohypothetical research traditions. Suffice it to say that we are now more conscious of the interface between our epistemological orientation and the dialectics of reflection in our research, and have thus become aware of a new set of discursive challenges facing us in this area (Lather, 1991).

REFERENCES

Adelman, C. (1984). *The politics and ethics of evaluation.* London: Croom Helm.

Alderson, J. C., & Beretta, A. (Eds.). (1992). *Evaluating second language education.* Cambridge, England: Cambridge University Press.

Bailey, K. M., & Nunan, D. (in press). *Voices from the language classroom: Qualitative research in language education.* New York: Cambridge University Press.

Beretta, A. (1992). What can be learned from The Bangalore Evaluation. In J. C. Alderson & A. Beretta (Eds.), *Evaluating second language education* (pp. 250–273). Cambridge, England: Cambridge University Press.

Bogdan, R., & Biklen, S. (1982). *Qualitative research for education.* Boston: Allyn & Bacon.

Breen, M. P. (1985). The social context for language learning—a neglected situation? *Studies in Second Language Acquisition, 7,* 135–158.

Campbell, R. N. (1989). Proposal to the United States Information Agency: Dual-language education. Language Resource Program, University of California, Los Angeles.

Carr, W., & Kemmis, S. (1986). *Becoming critical: Education, knowledge and action research*. London: Falmer Press.

Chaudron, C. (1988). *Second language classrooms: Research on teaching and learning*. Cambridge, England: Cambridge University Press.

Coleman, H. (1992). Moving the goalposts: Project evaluation in practice. In J. C. Alderson & A. Beretta (Eds.), *Evaluating second language education* (pp. 222–246). Cambridge, England: Cambridge University Press.

Coughlan, P., & Duff, P. (1994). Same task, different activities: Analysis of a SLA task from an activity theory perspective. In J. Lantolf & G. Appel (Eds.), *Vygotskian perspectives on second language research* (pp. 173–193). Norwood, NJ: Ablex.

Crandall, J. (1993). Content-centered learning in the United States. *Annual Review of Applied Linguistics, 13*, 111–126.

Crookes, G. (1993). Action research for second language teachers: Going beyond teacher research. *Applied Linguistics, 14*, 130–144.

Davis, K. A. (1995). Qualitative theory and methods in applied linguistics research. *TESOL Quarterly, 29*(3), 427–453.

Davis, K. A., & Lazaraton, A. (Eds.). (1995). Qualitative research in ESOL [special issue]. *TESOL Quarterly, 29*(3).

Duff, P. A. (1991). Innovations in foreign language education: An evaluation of three Hungarian-English dual-language programs. *Journal of Multilingual and Multicultural Development, 12*, 459–476.

Duff, P. A. (1993). *Changing times, changing minds: Language socialization in Hungarian-English schools*. Unpublished doctoral dissertation, University of California, Los Angeles.

Duff, P. A. (1995). An ethnography of communication in immersion classrooms in Hungary. *TESOL Quarterly, 29*(3), 505–537.

Duranti, A., & Goodwin, C. (Eds.). (1992). *Rethinking context*. Cambridge, England: Cambridge University Press.

Erickson, F. (1986). Qualitative methods in research on teaching. In M. Wittrock (Ed.), *Handbook of research on teaching (3rd ed.)* (pp. 119–161). New York: Macmillan.

Fisher, D. (1990). Field research and career education. In R. A. Young & W. A. Borgen (Eds.), *Methodological approaches to the study of career* (pp. 127–144). New York: Praeger.

Gal, S. (1989). Language and political economy. In B. J. Siegel, A. R. Beals, & S. A. Tyler (Eds.), *Annual review of anthropology*, (Vol. 18, pp. 345–367). Palo Alto: Annual Reviews.

Galloway, G., Marshall, S., Morgan, G., Muir, M. J., & Rooney, D. (1994). *In your classroom: Supporting the integration of secondary ESL learners*. Vancouver, BC: Vancouver School Board Curriculum Publications.

Gass, S. M., & Varonis, E. M. (1994). Input, interaction, and second language production. *Studies in Second Language Acquisition, 16*, 283–302.

Geertz, C. (1973). *The interpretation of cultures*. New York: Basic Books.

Guba, E. G., & Lincoln, Y. S. (1988). Do inquiry paradigms imply inquiry methodologies? In D. M. Fetterman (Ed.), *Qualitative approaches to evaluation in education* (pp. 89–115). New York: Praeger.

Guba, E. G., & Lincoln, Y. S. (1989). *Fourth generation evaluation.* London: Sage.

Hatch, E., & Hawkins, B. (1987). Second language acquisition: An experiential approach. In S. Rosenthal (Ed.), *Advances in applied psycholinguistics: Vol. 2. Reading, writing and language learning* (pp. 241–283). Cambridge, England: Cambridge University Press.

Hatch, E., & Lazaraton, A. (1991). *The research manual: Design and statistics for applied linguistics.* New York: Newbury House.

Hopkins, D. (1989). *Evaluation for school development.* Milton Keynes, UK: Open University Press.

Johnson, D. (1992). *Approaches to research in second language learning.* New York: Longman.

Kramsch, C. (1993). *Context and culture in language teaching.* Oxford, England: Oxford University Press.

Lantolf, J., & Appel, G. (Eds.). (1994). *Vygotskian approaches to second language research.* New Jersey: Ablex.

Larsen-Freeman, D., & Long, M. H. (1991). *An introduction to second language acquisition research.* London: Longman.

Lather, P. (1991). *Getting smart: Feminist research and pedagogy with/in the postmodern.* New York: Routledge, Chapman and Hall.

Lave, J. (1988). *Cognition in practice: Mind, mathematics, and culture in everyday life.* Cambridge, England: Cambridge University Press.

Lave, J., & Wenger, E. (1991). *Situated learning: Legitimate peripheral participation.* Cambridge, England: Cambridge University Press.

Lazaraton, A. (1995). Qualitative research in applied linguistics: A progress report. *TESOL Quarterly, 29*(3), 455–472.

LeCompte, M. D., & Preissle, J. (with Tesch, R.). (1993). *Ethnography and qualitative design in education.* New York: Academic Press.

Lightbown, P. M., Spada, N., & White, L. (Eds.) (1993). The role of instruction in second language acquisition [special issue]. *Studies in Second Language Acquisition, 15, 2.*

Long, M. H. (1983). Does second language instruction make a difference? A review of research. *TESOL Quarterly, 17,* 359–382.

Loschky, L. (1994). Comprehensible input and second language acquisition: What is the relationship? *Studies in Second Language Acquisition, 16,* 303–323.

Miles, M. B., & Huberman, A. M. (1984). *Qualitative data analysis.* Newbury Park, CA: Sage.

Miles, M. B., & Huberman, A. M. (1988). Drawing valid meaning from qualitative data: Toward a shared craft. In D. M. Fetterman (Ed.), *Qualitative approaches to evaluation in education* (pp. 222–244). New York: Praeger.

Mitchell, R. (1985). Process research in second-language classrooms. *Language Teaching, 18,* 330–352.

Mohan, B. (1986). *Language and content.* Reading, MA: Addison-Wesley.

Nunan, D. (1990). Action research in the language classroom. In J. Richards & D. Nunan (Eds.), *Second language teacher education* (pp.

62–81). Cambridge, England: Cambridge University Press.

Nunan, D. (1992). *Research methods in language learning*. Cambridge, England: Cambridge University Press.

Ochs, E. (1979). Transcription as theory. In E. Ochs & B. Schieffelin (Eds.), *Developmental pragmatics* (pp. 43–72). New York: Academic Press.

Ogbu, J. U. (1982). Cultural discontinuities and schooling. *Anthropology and Education Quarterly, 13*, 290–307.

Patton, M. Q. (1988). Paradigms and pragmatism. In D. M. Fetterman (Ed.), *Qualitative approaches to evaluation in education* (pp. 116–137). New York: Praeger.

Pennycook, A. (1990). Towards a critical applied linguistics for the 1990s. *Issues in Applied Linguistics, 1*, 8–28.

Reichardt, C., & Cook, T. (1979). Beyond qualitative versus quantitative methods. In T. Cook & C. Reichardt (Eds.), *Qualitative and quantitative methods in evaluation research* (pp. 7–32). Beverly Hills, CA: Sage.

Rogoff, B. (1990). *Apprenticeship in thinking*. New York: Oxford University Press.

Seliger, H., & Shohamy, E. (1989). *Second language research methods*. Oxford, England: Oxford University Press.

Sullivan, B. (1988). *The report of the Royal Commission on Education: A legacy for learners*. Victoria, Canada: Province of British Columbia.

Swain, M. (1995, March). *Collaborative dialogue: Its contribution to second language learning*. Plenary paper presented at the annual meeting of the American Association for Applied Linguistics, Long Beach, CA.

Swain, M., & Cumming, A. (1989). Beyond methodology: Behind research. In J. H. Esling (Ed.), *Multicultural education and policy: ESL in the 1990s* (pp. 88–106). Toronto: OISE Press.

Ulichny, P. (1989). *Exploring a teacher's practice: Collaborative research in an adult ESL reading class*. Unpublished doctoral dissertation, Harvard University.

van Lier, L. (1988). *The classroom and the language learner*. New York: Longman.

Watson-Gegeo, K. A. (1988). Ethnography in ESL: Defining the essentials. *TESOL Quarterly, 22*, 575–592.

Wells, G., & Chang-Wells, G-L. (1992). *Constructing knowledge together*. Portsmouth, NH: Heinemann.

Willett, J. (1995). Becoming first graders in an L2: An ethnographic study of L2 socialization. *TESOL Quarterly, 29*(3), 473–503.

Chapter 2

Working with Teachers in Second Language Acquisition Research

Nina Spada
McGill University

Leila Ranta
Patsy M. Lightbown
Concordia University

Since the late 1970s, members of our research group have been actively involved in classroom research in several second language (L2) teaching/learning environments. During this time, we have worked closely with many classroom teachers. Our purpose in this chapter is to describe how we have involved and interacted with teachers in our investigations of the relationship between teaching and learning in L2 classrooms. We begin by providing a brief description of the educational context in which most of our recent research has taken place.

RESEARCH CONTEXT

A particular focus of our research group since the mid-1980s has been intensive English as a second language (ESL) classes in the French language primary schools in the province of Quebec. In these programs, young francophone students receive full days of ESL instruction 5 days a week for 5 months of one school year, in either grade 5 or 6. The other 5 months are spent studying the regular French and math curriculum for the grade level. These intensive programs differ from immersion programs in that no subject matter is taught through the second language, and students can only enroll in them once during their primary school education. For these 5 months, they receive intensive communicative exposure to English. Afterwards, students return to the regular ESL program.[1] Although the regular program is also communicative in nature, the amount of instruction learners receive in the intensive programs contrasts markedly with the regular program, which allots no more than 2 hours a week to ESL instruction. Intensive ESL classes began in a few school boards some 15 years ago and are now found in many parts of Quebec, although the vast majority of French speaking students continue to receive the regular "drip-feed" type of ESL instruction (see Lightbown & Spada, 1994, for a more complete description of the intensive ESL programs).

Our research in the intensive programs has focused on the description of the ESL development of learners and the type of instruction they receive. We have also investigated the extent to which differences in instruction contribute to differences in learning outcomes as well as the contributions that such programs make to the learners' attitudes toward and contact with English. We have been particularly interested in examining whether and in what ways the inclusion of form-focused instruction and error correction within these communicative programs contributes to the English language development of the learners. Several papers reporting the results of our research have been published in research and professional journals.[2]

This chapter represents a shift away from descriptions of the learners, their language, and the type of instruction

---

[1]Recently, some school boards have created special programs for postintensive students, but this was not true of most school boards prior to 1990.

[2]Because the focus of this chapter is the involvement of teachers in research in the intensive programs, no details regarding the specific findings of individual studies are reported here. Instead, these publications are cited in the appropriate sections and complete references are included in the reference list. A project bibliography may also be made available upon request.

they receive, to a discussion of the teachers and more specifically, to a description of how we have involved them in our classroom research. Teachers who are willing to welcome researchers into their classrooms are invaluable participants in the research effort. Without their cooperation, no classroom-centered research could be done. Approaching teachers as respected colleagues rather than merely as sources of data for a distant research endeavour is of crucial importance.

When we were first asked to organize our chapter around the question "How did you get teachers to participate in classroom experiments?" our first response was deceptively simple — "Well, we asked them and they said, 'When would you like to come?'" As we began to reflect on the process of how this was accomplished, however, and examined particular aspects of our work before, during, and after research in these programs, it became clear that it was not quite as simple as we had originally thought. Years of work went into establishing and maintaining the connections and cooperation between our research group and the teachers in the schools. This chapter outlines those factors which we feel have contributed most to this relationship, including a discussion of how we made decisions about the selection of teachers for particular studies, the manner and extent to which we informed them about the theoretical issues and research questions under investigation, how we engaged teachers in the research process, what mechanisms we developed for feedback to the teachers and school boards, external factors that operated in our favor, and perhaps most importantly, how crucial links (formal and informal) established at various professional and academic levels contributed significantly to the process of building a cooperative and interactive relationship between researchers and teachers.

We should acknowledge at the outset that one of the advantages we experienced was that the intensive programs were new and innovative when we began our research in them. Indeed, they are still considered to be experimental by the Quebec Ministry of Education. As a result, these programs have attracted considerable interest on the part of parents, teachers, school boards and ministry officials who are interested in determining how learners' English language abilities develop and how they compare with learners in the regular ESL programs. It is also important to point out that the majority of teachers in the intensive program are a particularly motivated and highly committed group of professionals.

Because our work in this context has evolved as a research cycle of description, correlation, and experimentation, we have organized the chapter within this framework to describe the involvement of teachers at various phases of the research cycle.[3] There were also factors in the preresearch phase which are important to note and these will be outlined first.

Preresearch Phase

Our research in the intensive program classes began in the mid-1980s when a classroom teacher approached one of the members of our research team to tell her about the exciting new ESL program at her school. She wanted to determine whether it would be possible for the researcher to become involved in some preliminary evaluations of it. The teacher came to the university because she knew of the researcher's active involvement at teachers' meetings and her contributions to publications read by teachers. She was also known to support communicative language teaching on the basis of her research in audiolingual ESL classes in the late 1970s. This meeting marked the beginning of a positive relationship that we have continued to enjoy with the intensive program teachers and students ever since. An important component of this is undoubtedly linked to the fact that it was the teachers who opened the door for us. That is, we were not in the position of having to sell an interesting research idea to a group of teachers or a school board, at least not initially. Rather, the teachers, parents, and school board administrators had several important questions they called on our research group to help investi-

---

[3]The three elements of description, correlation, and experimentation were initially proposed by Rosenshine and Furst (1973) in a model for studying teaching and learning in first language classrooms.

gate. After some preliminary work in these programs, we began to develop our own set of research questions and hypotheses, some of which were considered to be less relevant or interesting to the teachers. This presented greater challenges for us as we became more involved in the process of undertaking research that could accommodate our agenda as researchers and theirs as classroom practitioners.

Phase I: Description

Following a few small-scale pilot studies from 1984-1985, a 3 year study was launched. The first requirement for research in these new programs was a description of both classroom practice and learning outcomes. For 3 years, we observed teachers teaching and learners learning in many intensive ESL classrooms in different parts of Quebec. Our classroom observations were structured by a scheme referred to as COLT (communicative orientation of language teaching), which one of the members of our team had developed with her colleagues in earlier classroom research (Allen, Fröhlich, & Spada, 1984; Fröhlich, Spada, & Allen, 1985; Spada & Fröhlich, 1995). We used this scheme to systematically observe and describe the instructional practices in terms of the type of activities, the amount of listening, reading, speaking, and writing that took place, the extent to which instruction was teacher-centered or learner-centered, and the extent to which teachers corrected learners' errors or taught grammar. These descriptions were supplemented by audiorecordings of classroom interaction which were reviewed and transcribed for further, more detailed analysis. To obtain a description of learning outcomes, we administered group listening comprehension tests and collected samples of oral production from individual students. Throughout, we tried our best not to interfere in classroom interaction except by our very presence, which students and teachers soon learned to ignore or to make use of for interviews, guessing games, or just to have an additional English speaker in ongoing classroom activities.

In hindsight, we have come to realize how much this period of silent observation contributed to the development of feelings of trust between teachers and researchers. This was accomplished in a variety of ways. We were present in the classrooms for full days including lunch hours and recess. This created an opportunity for a continuing dialogue between teachers and researchers. The teachers talked to us about their interests and goals and we were available to respond to questions they had about our observations. We discussed a wide range of issues concerning L2 teaching and learning. This phase of our work also enabled us to provide the teachers and school boards with information they needed regarding the English language performance of their students. We made every effort to score and analyze the results of the language tests as quickly as possible, and the information was provided to the teachers and school boards in a relatively jargon-free manner. We reported the results of our observational research at local teachers' conferences, attended the intensive program teachers' meetings during these conferences and, where possible and appropriate, responded to the particular requests of individual school boards. Sometimes our graduate student assistants undertook specific projects in the intensive programs as part of their academic training. In one case, a school board requested an objective evaluation of their intensive program teaching materials. One of our master's level students with a particular interest in curriculum and materials evaluation completed this project as part of the requirements for her degree (Weary, 1987). In other cases, our research assistants were called on to provide oral testing of ESL students who had completed an intensive program.

The descriptive phase of our research revealed that the English language development of learners in intensive ESL far exceeded that of learners at the same grade level in the regular ESL programs and of older learners who had received a comparable amount of English language instruction over a longer period of time. Our classroom observations confirmed that overall, these learners received a steady diet of communicative instruction in which the focus was on meaning with little attention given to accuracy and grammar. We also noticed, however, that some teachers tended to spend a little more time on form and accuracy within the context of communicative activities (see Spada, 1990a,

1990b; Spada & Lightbown, 1989 for details). This led into the next phase of our research.

Phase II: Correlation

Although we have labelled this as correlation, it is important to note that we are not using the term in the statistical sense, but rather, in an informal manner to characterize a period during which we qualitatively investigated potential relationships between classroom instruction and learner language data. For example, we wondered whether learners in those classes where the teachers focused more on form and accuracy (within an overall communicative context) benefited from this type of instruction. There was evidence that they did (see Lightbown, 1991; Lightbown & Spada, 1990 for details).

When we discovered this relationship, we began to talk about it with teachers. At the same time we gave presentations at local teachers' conferences about the potential benefits of including some attention to form and accuracy within communicative programs. This was a particularly challenging period in the research process because many of the intensive program teachers were convinced that an exclusive focus on meaning was the most appropriate and beneficial approach, and there was strong resistance to the inclusion of any attention to error correction or grammatical instruction. Much discussion and dialogue took place at this time. We had to reassure teachers that our hypotheses (based on the preliminary findings) were not leading us to advocate a return to the structure-based audiolingual approach involving meaningless drill and constant correction which was typical of many Quebec ESL classes before 1980. Rather, we were interested in investigating in a more controlled and systematic manner whether the inclusion of some focus on form and error correction within a communicative approach would help learners develop higher levels of performance and accuracy, without diminishing their confidence and fluency. In the end, through discussion, clarification, and ongoing dialogue, we obtained the agreement of some teachers that this idea merited investigation. This led to the next phase of our research.

Phase III: Experimentation

During this period, we carried out a series of quasiexperimental[4] studies to test the hypothesis that a greater focus on form and error correction in these highly communicative classes would be beneficial. The studies consisted of a comparison between those classes that received form-focused teaching and error correction on specific linguistic structures, and those that did not. In this phase it was essential to work closely with the teachers to ensure that the teaching experiments across classes were carried out consistently. This led to a number of decisions concerning the selection of teachers, the implementation of the teaching materials, and the distribution of results.

Selection of Teachers. In a true experimental design, the subjects (i.e., teachers and students) are randomly assigned to either a treatment or control condition. In our experience, in the world of real schools, real teachers, and real students, this almost never happens. First, we almost always find it necessary to work with intact classes. Furthermore, in light of guidelines for ethical research practices, we can only work with those who are willing to participate. We try to select teachers whose characteristics and previous teaching behaviors match the goals of a particular study. For example, in one of our studies on the teaching of adverb placement, we chose to work only with teachers who were native speakers of English. Rules for adverb placement differ in French and English, and it is an enduring problem even for many advanced francophone speakers of English. In selecting only native speakers for both the treatment and comparison groups, we hoped to control for the possibility that nonnative speaking teachers might not react to learners' errors or might even provide learners with inappropriate input in their own speech (see Trahey, 1992; Trahey & White, 1993; White, 1991, for details). To cite another example, in one of our experimental studies on the

---

[4]The label *quasiexperimental* (as opposed to *experimental*) is used here because this research did not involve randomly assigning students to different treatment groups as is the case in experimental research.

development of question formation, we assigned the no form-focus condition to a teacher who was very explicit about her dislike for teaching grammar thus assuring ourselves of a pure uninstructed group to compare with those who were using the form-focus materials we had prepared.

Such decisions limit the generalizability of the findings because it can never be ruled out that a selection criterion rather than the treatment alone was responsible for the results. A partial compensation for the necessity of working with intact classes is to use fairly extensive pretests and questionnaires in order to establish the similarity of groups prior to the experimental intervention. One way to partly offset the problem of teacher differences is to gather as much pertinent information as possible about the teachers' classroom language and teaching style so that the results can be contextualized. The importance of having this information is not to be underestimated. The one time that we chose a teacher at random without prior observation taught us an important lesson. She was to be the teacher in the no form-focus comparison group, but we found to our surprise that her teaching style represented an even stronger version of the form-focus and corrective feedback profile we had implemented in the experimental classes (see Spada & Lightbown, 1993).

In preparation for future research, we have developed a questionnaire about the teaching styles of prospective participating teachers. In addition, we will do observations in each classroom prior to introducing experimental treatments. This will be necessary even when we are working with teachers we know well. As experienced teachers and classroom researchers know, teachers not only change over time, but they also interact differently with different groups of students.

Implementation of Materials.   Once we have selected the teachers and obtained their permission to carry out the experiments in their classes, the next step is to provide direction and guidance in the implementation of the instructional treatment. This leads to other important decisions and some inevitable trade-offs. In the adverb and question formation studies, it was decided not to give a training session in the use of materials prior to the study. This decision was based on our wish to work with teachers who were blind to the experimental goals. That is, we did not want the teachers to know in advance what particular aspects of language were under investigation to avoid the possibility that teachers' heightened awareness of these forms might draw their attention to them, thus affecting student performance on the pretests. There are some drawbacks to this decision, however, one being that it did not permit us to gain information from the teachers before the experiment concerning their interest in or their prior behavior toward the target structures. In fact, we discovered on the first day of the question formation experiment that one teacher had taught his class that "may" must be used for asking permission, whereas our instructional materials introduced "can" in this context. In an effort to avoid this particular problem, our most recent work has involved a much closer collaboration with the teachers concerned. Thus, in one study, teachers were informed about the object of the study, and they decided among themselves (i.e., separately from the researcher) which teacher would be teaching which of the three treatments (see White, 1995, for details).

Another potentially serious drawback to not providing training sessions for experimental teachers is that it can lead to inconsistencies in the use of the teaching materials. We have taken a number of steps in an effort to obtain as much consistency as possible in the appropriate implementation of the instructional materials. We provide detailed instructions and guidelines for the teachers on the use of the materials, their order of presentation, and the amount of time to be spent on each activity. To ensure more uniformity, we also provide the teachers with all the material they need for themselves, their students, and the classroom while teaching the instructional unit. This includes posters for the classroom walls, copies of all exercises and handouts for students, cards and pictures for various activities, and so forth. Furthermore, while the experiments are underway, teachers are asked to keep daily logs of how much time they spend on the materials, exercises, and activities, and to indicate what changes and deletions they make. They are also encouraged to call us at any time if they have questions or are uncertain about any aspect of the teaching materials. As a final check on the implementation of the materials, the teachers are asked to audiorecord their classes while the experimental materials are being used.

As indicated above, we have sometimes withheld information about the research from the teachers directly involved in the experimental studies. However, we have involved other intensive program teachers in the preparation of the research for them. In order to ensure that the instructional materials are at an appropriate level of interest and difficulty for the learners, some intensive program teachers have participated regularly in the development of the materials. In one case, a teacher was hired to develop the materials for a study. In another case, a research assistant developed the materials first and then worked together with a teacher who read them and made suggestions for revisions. We have also received the cooperation and involvement of intensive program teachers in pilot testing some of the learner language measures. Sometimes these teachers were our former students.

Reporting Findings to Teachers. The reporting process is another important facet of doing research in classrooms that is often overlooked. Informing teachers about the results of research requires a delicate balance. It is certainly inappropriate to point an accusing finger or to dictate to teachers how they should teach on the basis of what one has discovered. On the other hand, teachers who have been willing to accept extra work or inconvenience clearly deserve to know what has come from their efforts. Indeed, ethical guidelines for all research with human subjects quite rightly require this.

Our approach to disseminating the results of research takes several different forms. In many instances, summary reports of the research, which are presented in accessible formats, have been distributed to the schools and school boards. Our preference is to present the results of research in a neutral environment such as teachers' conventions and newsletters, couched in terms that are purposely both anonymous and tentative (see Polio, chapter 4). Because many members of the research group are associated with

teacher training departments, we have further opportunities to disseminate research findings to teachers-in-train-
ing, as well as to experienced teachers through in-service
workshops. In doing so, we are careful to point out the limitations of our research and to recognize that whatever suggestions we might have for pedagogical change form part of
a dialogue between us and the teachers. For instance, one
of our concerns was that there was insufficient time spent
on reading and writing in the intensive ESL classes. We
began to talk with teachers about this and some who shared
this concern decided to participate in a study with one of
the members of our team to investigate how the provision
of more reading might benefit the students (see Goulet &
White, 1993; White, 1995).

We are also careful to acknowledge to teachers that our
research has focused only on some specific aspects of teaching in their classes, although they are faced with a constel-
lation of factors that must be considered when making informed decisions about what is best for their students and
their programs. We emphasize our awareness that the teachers have a great deal of knowledge and experience for us to
draw from. This enables us to interact with them as colleagues and as a result, this sometimes leads them (and
other school personnel) to initiate research ideas. A recent
example of this comes from one school in which the intensive ESL program includes opportunities for students to use
English throughout the school day – in the corridors, on
the playground, in the cafeteria, and so forth. The personnel of this school have asked us to investigate the effectiveness of this extended use of and exposure to English within
the school.

CONCLUSION

In this chapter, we have outlined several factors which we
believe have contributed to the successful involvement of
teachers in our research in second language classrooms.
We have learned a great deal from this experience. Upon
reflection, we have come to realize the importance of our
involvement in a variety of professional activities, which have

enabled us to establish and maintain a productive and co-operative relationship with these teachers over an extended period of time. These include teaching courses in language acquisition and teaching methodology to student teachers, giving workshops, and doing committee work with the local ESL teachers' association, consulting on curriculum with the Ministry of Education, and publishing in professional as well as scholarly journals. All these activities have contributed to our ability to work successfully with teachers.

Two guiding principles from our experience may be helpful to others who are embarking upon a program of classroom research: (1) Build trust in prospective participating teachers before asking them for favors, and (2) Obtain as much information as possible about how the teachers teach before involving them in an experiment. Because it is possible to do both by watching and listening, we strongly recommend beginning every study with a period of classroom observation.

ACKNOWLEDGMENTS

Funding for this research has been provided by the Social Sciences and Humanities Research Council of Canada and by the Quebec Ministry of Education's research funding agency (Fonds pour la formation de chercheurs et l'aide à la recherche). We wish to thank the teachers for their generosity, support, and commitment. We are also grateful to our research assistants for their excellent work in all phases of this research.

REFERENCES

Allen, J. P. B., Fröhlich M., & Spada N., (1984). The communicative orientation of second language teaching: An observation scheme. In J. Handscombe, R. Orem, & B. Taylor (Eds.), *On TESOL '83*, (pp. 231–252). Washington, DC: TESOL.

Fröhlich, M., Spada, N., & Allen, P. (1985). Differences in the communicative orientation of L2 classrooms. *TESOL Quarterly*, *19*(1), 27–57.

Goulet, C., & White, J. (1993, October). *What! They're reading again! A book flood project in a grade 6 intensive class.* Paper presented at the

Twenty-first SPEAQ conference. Montreal.

Lightbown, P. M. (1991). What have we here? Some observations on the influence of instruction on L2 learning. In R. Phillipson, E. Kellerman, L. Selinker, M. Sharwood Smith, & M. Swain (eds.), *Foreign language pedagogy research: A commemorative volume for Claus Faerch* (pp. 197–212). Clevedon, *Multilingual Matters*.

Lightbown, P. M., & Spada, N. (1990). Focus on form and corrective feedback in communicative language teaching: Effects on second language learning. *Studies in Second Language Acquisition, 12*(4), 429–448.

Lightbown, P. M., & Spada, N. (1994). An innovative program for primary ESL in Quebec. *TESOL Quarterly, 23*(3), 563–579.

Rosenshine, B., & Furst, N. (1973). The use of direct observation to study teaching. In R. Travers (Ed.), *Second handbook of research on teaching* (122–183). Chicago: Rand McNally.

Spada, N. (1990a). A look at the research process in classroom observation: A case study. In C. Brumfit & R. Mitchell (Eds.), *ELT Documents: Research in the language classroom* (pp. 81–93). London: Modern English Publications.

Spada, N. (1990b). Observing classroom behaviors and learning outcomes in different second language programs. In J.C. Richards & D. Nunan (eds.), *Second language Teacher education: Content and process* (pp. 293–310). New York: Cambridge University Press.

Spada, N., & Fröhlich, M. (1995) *The communicative orientation of language teaching (COLT) observation scheme: Coding Conventions and Applications*. Manuscript in progress. Macquarie University, Sydney, Australia.

Spada, N., & Lightbown, P. M. (1989). Intensive ESL programs in Quebec primary schools. *TESL Canada Journal, 7*(1), 11–32.

Spada, N., & Lightbown, P. M. (1993). Instruction and the development of questions in L2 classrooms. *Studies in Second Language Acquisition, 15*(2), 205–224.

Trahey, M. (1992). *Comprehensible input and second language acquisition*. Unpublished master's thesis, McGill University, Montreal.

Trahey, M., & White, L. (1993). Positive evidence and preemption in the second language classroom. *Studies in Second Language Acquisition, 15*(2), 181–204.

Weary, K. (1987). *An evaluation of the pedagogical materials of an intensive ESL program at the grade 6 level*. Unpublished master's thesis, McGill University, Montreal.

White, J. (1995, March). *Getting the learners' attention: A typographical input enhancement study*. Paper presented at the meeting of the American Association for Applied Linguistics, Long Beach, CA.

White, L. (1991). Adverb placement in second language acquisition: Some effects of positive and negative evidence in the classroom. *Second Language Research, 7*, 133–161.

Chapter 3

The Classroom-Based Researcher as Fieldworker: Strangers in a Strange Land

Patricia L. Rounds
University of Oregon

There are considerable and numerous obstacles to system-atic classroom-based language learning research due to the complex nature of the classroom environment: Learners often have varying native languages and cultures, proficiency levels, learning styles, motivations, and attitudes; teachers have their own distinctive belief systems, teaching styles, preferred language, teaching materials, and professional and personal agendas. Furthermore, the work of these teachers and learners takes place in educational institutions that have their own sets of political, financial, educational, and social concerns. The goal of carrying out systematic and theoretically sound classroom studies can give rise to con-flict between researcher and school personnel, leading to anything from minor personal friction to skewed results or aborted research plans.

What is the source of this friction? Researchers often describe the teachers they study as uncooperative, unhelp-ful, inflexible, untrusting, and even just plain obstruction-ist. How is it that researchers are sometimes seen by these same teachers as being demanding, intrusive, unhelpful, inflexible, and dogmatic? This is the group of questions I intend to consider here: a range of issues related to the complexities of the classroom community. My focus is on the very practical day-to-day problems that arise when people interact.

THE SETTING

My fieldworker-based view of this group of problems is grounded in a classroom-based language learning project I supervised a few years ago. In general it was a rewarding and insightful experience; however, there were moments when my students and I wondered what was going on and where we had gone wrong.

I had been asked to teach a seminar on child second lan-guage development using a local immersion school as a re-search site. The term immersion is used in our school dis-trict to describe educational programs in which elementary through high school, mostly native English speaking stu-dents, receive half of their instruction each day in English and half of it in a foreign language, either French, Spanish, or Japanese. I was asked to teach this course because the school district was interested in accessing the expertise of the university to further the development of this particular program, and the university was interested in strengthen-ing the ties between it and the local community. I agreed to do it because I thought the combination of a theoretically based seminar coupled with an opportunity for university applied linguistics students to actually observe language teaching and learning development seemed ideal.

After several days of observing classes and meeting with the teachers, in consultation with the principal, I devised a simple project that we thought might achieve some mea-sure of success and that would be useful to the school: The seminar students would videotape each grade level through an entire day. This would provide the archival record that the principal wanted of this innovative program and it would get the relatively untrained seminar students into the class-rooms where the business of teaching and learning were taking place. The seminar students would then use these tapes to produce an edited tape representative of the activities of the day. In order to produce such a tape, they would need to carefully articulate and analyze the day's activities in terms of education, in general, and second language development, in particular. In order to develop an understanding of the classroom activities, we planned to use the ethnographic strategy of triangulation, which included not only our own observations and perceptions, but also the comments from the participants, in this case the teachers and students, on the classroom activities. We felt that this phase of the project would publicly recognize the teachers and students as experts, thus making them part of the research or the "learning about learning" process, while giving us information about the belief systems of the participants in the educational process. We planned to use representative excerpts of the teachers' and students' comments as voice-over for the edited tapes.

This seemed to us to be a fairly benign project. Given that the immersion students were already accustomed to being observed and videotaped, we all felt that making another tape was a relatively unobtrusive proposal. Because this was to be a "typical" day, we intended for it not to be an added burden to the teachers in terms of planning and preparation. A meeting was called to discuss our proposal with the teachers. The teachers were polite; some were even enthusiastic. There was some discussion about exact goals and time frame, but they all agreed to participate.

At the beginning of the semester, the seminar students made personal contact with the teachers to set up a day to do the videotaping and visited the school to make sure they had an understanding of the classroom set ups. Everything went off without any perceivable hitch.

However, when we came to the part of the project that required the teachers to review the tapes, problems began to surface. First of all, some of the teachers were unhappy about being interviewed about their classes. Somehow the word "interview" was interpreted in this context as "inquisition." At first, it seemed that we only needed to agree on another term to index this activity. However, when we tried to track how an interview could become an inquisition, it became clear that such a view could easily be ascribed to our activities. Both activities have data gathering as a main goal with the difference being the intended use of the data. Inquisition certainly implies underlying hostile intent. The teachers had no reason to believe that our motives were simply the acquisition of knowledge for its own sake; in fact, it makes much more sense to gather information for a purpose. Our motives were not clear; we were not absolutely trusted.

A more serious problem from a research perspective surfaced when the seminar students asked one of the teachers to review the tape of her classes (each teacher taught a morning and an afternoon session). She replied that she had already put in enough time on this project and she did not have any more time to spend on it as she had a considerable amount of work to do in order to prepare the students for an official visit from a group of dignitaries the following week. When the seminar students appeared puzzled (after all this was supposed to be a typical day, and we had intended that nothing out of the ordinary should be prepared), the teacher pointed out how much extra preparation she had had because of our project, and how much it had interfered with her previously projected plans for that day.

We wondered what we had captured of a typical day. What, if anything, was typical? In our seminar discussion we noticed how disciplined those classes were, and how the students had very few opportunities to create language. Their time in the second language seemed to us to be devoted to rote responses. (Jennifer, what color is the seed? White. Mark, what color is the seed? White.) Was this normal, or a strategy the teacher used for that day so that we would see the students perform in the language? If it was normal, what could we, as students interested in the processes of second language acquisition, say about how these students were learning? After all, we were disciples of the methodological school which advocates providing early and frequent opportunities to create language. We could, of course, get more data by going back to the classes and doing some long-term observing, but these options were not within the purview of this particular project.

But this story is not yet over. After this teacher declined to review the tapes, the other members of her teaching team were approached and enthusiastically decided to spend some time over the weekend reviewing and commenting on the tapes of their classes. In fact, they planned to do it together and do it at the home of their reluctant colleague! In the end, to satisfy her fellow teachers and the seminar students, this teacher wrote out a script that she carefully read into a tape recorder. She suggested that we could use the same tape for both her classes. So much, we thought, for grounded insight and analysis!

We were clearly frustrated and, yet, even more than that, we were puzzled. Where had we gone wrong? Why wasn't this teacher interested in how we could help her do her job better? Was she just being uncooperative, unhelpful, inflexible, untrusting, and even just plain obstructionist? This didn't seem to be a productive standpoint for us to take. But neither could we warm up to the view that we were being demanding, intrusive, unhelpful, inflexible, and dogmatic.

In 1980, the TESOL Research Committee published a set of "Guidelines for Ethical Research in ESL" in the *TESOL Quarterly* (Tarone, 1980). This set of guidelines states very strongly that, "All research on humans should proceed only with the uncoerced, informed consent of the subjects, in writing if possible" (p. 384). Of course we did that. But what kind of permission did we really get? Did we coerce this teacher?

In our seminar, we tried hard to understand our project and our related needs from this particular teacher's point of view, not only to deal more sensitively with her, but also because she might represent the unspoken feelings of other, shyer, teachers. Our intentions were straightforward: We needed to see a typical day. But, we were also aware that what was typical for these classrooms had been negatively criticized by an earlier group of consultants; we could certainly be construed as another group of potential critics. Thus, we threatened her professional status. We needed to ask questions. Being bombarded with questions could easily take on more of the tenor of an inquisition than a benign interview. We needed this teacher to go on record describing her classes. We realized she was (unnecessarily in our minds) tremendously self-conscious about her English pro-

ficiency, yet, we were asking her to expose her perceived
language deficit to all comers. Thus, we threatened her personal image. Maybe most importantly we needed her time.
We eventually came to appreciate that she had to develop
and teach a program that was at the very least challenging,
and also somehow prepare the students to entertain some
important visitors. Clearly and reasonably, from her point
of view, our needs did not even come close to matching her
needs. We became, appropriately, a low priority, a nuisance.

THE LESSON

Goffman (1961, pp. ix-x) said, "any group of persons—pris-
oners, primitives, pilots, or patients—develops a life of their
own that becomes meaningful, reasonable, and normal once
you get close to it."

The group of persons which make up a school or a classroom develops a life, a society that is meaningful, reasonable, and normal to them. It is a society encompassing ritual,
hierarchy, role relationships, status—all the features that
make up any traditional society. I have come to believe that
if we hope to do a good job at classroom research we need
to recognize this fact and see ourselves in the same way
that anthropological fieldworkers see themselves: as visitors, or as strangers in a strange land.

The traditional goal of fieldwork is to go into little known,
often strange or exotic, social worlds, and to describe these
worlds in ways that make their inhabitants' beliefs and practices comprehensible to others, that is, outsiders. Classroom-based researchers are much like these traditional anthropological fieldworkers; both leave the safe haven of
academia to study other peoples. This is not the world of
laboratory-based experiments where we are, in a sense, at
home; nor are we conducting experiments where we invite
others to come to our turf, where the pressure is on them to
perform, where we can attach electrodes to their brains and
measure their behaviors through supposedly objective or
nonemotional observation. In fieldwork or classroom-based
research we are out there on their turf. The pressure is on
us to get their approval and cooperation. We do not have
any power to make things happen to suit us. But if we try to

conceptualize the school where we carry out our classroom-based research in the same way as an anthropologist must conceptualize a village in a foreign culture she intends to study, I believe we will better understand the behavior of some of its inhabitants, and better understand the nature of the relationship and responsibilities between researchers and the researched.

First of all, we need to understand who all the inhabitants of our targeted village are, and their roles in the village. A fieldwork analogy may prove useful. For example, in the case I have been describing, we have, in a sense, a national government (i.e., school district administrators) that has invited a foreign guest (i.e., applied linguist) to study one of its remote villages (i.e., an immersion school). The village head (i.e., principal) has agreed to allow the foreign guest to reside in her village. A town meeting is called and the leading citizens (i.e., faculty) are asked to extend hospitality to the guest. They agree for the sake of village unity.

Now let us consider the motives or goals of a national government (school district). Why is it being so cooperative? Does it perceive benefit in terms of money or publicity? Does it need some information about possibly subversive groups in the village?

What are the motives of the village head (principal)? Is she trying to curry favor with the national government? Does she hope to become the foreign guest's most favored person, and thereby accrue some personal benefit from that guest? Or is she just interested in progress, development, and integrating her village into modern society?

How much will the citizenry (teachers and students) be inconvenienced? Will the foreign guest sleep on the floor of someone's hut (just observe a typical day) or will the populace be required to build her a new house (do something out of the ordinary)? Who will take care of her needs (research), feed her (answer interview questions), wash her clothes (comment on videotapes)?

What benefit accrues to the village population at large? Will they get some public improvement from foreign funds provided by the researcher? Or will the information gathered be used to harm them in some way as yet unknown to them?

Who will ultimately use the information gathered? The

national government? Some group of researchers who will put the culture under the microscope and dissect the behaviors of these strange creatures? And what of their village reputation? Will their dirty laundry be hung out for the country's scrutiny?

Once we began to perceive ourselves in this way in our seminar, the so-called problems we ran up against took on a different light. This light was revealing. Viewing ourselves from this perspective helped us see the situation not as a peculiar clash of personalities and politics, but as a cross-cultural experience that needed to be treated with all the sensitivity and forethought that traditional fieldwork demands and that few of us are taught to supply. Furthermore, if we accept this conceptualization of ourselves as fieldworkers as a valid conceptualization, we begin to realize more clearly that the information we gather can have powerful and perhaps threatening effects on those we study. We also should realize that when granted the right to get information, we take on certain responsibilities.

THREE FRAMEWORKS FOR CONSCIOUSNESS RAISING: HOW WE SEE AND GOVERN OUR ACTIONS

What connects anthropology, linguistics, and other social sciences is that their primary data come from objects who talk back. These objects have opinions about themselves, opinions about the social scientists who work among them, and explanations of their own behavior. These objects of course possess the right and ability to protect themselves. In the case described here, the school eventually published its own set of guidelines for researchers. But I think we have a responsibility to be proactive in our thinking about how we ought to interact with the citizens of the communities we study.

Cameron, Frazer, Harvey, Rampton, and Richardson (1993) alluded to a fact that most anthropological fieldworkers are well aware of: Power relations exist in fieldwork situations, and this unequal relationship usually benefits the researcher more than the researched. However, they pointed out that this inequality is not necessarily a result of preexisting status differences, but that the act of doing research causes this disparity. They examined the assumptions and practices social scientists work within when they go into the field and identified three frameworks for under-standing the forces that influence the developing relation-ships between researchers and their subjects: the ethics, the advocacy, and the empowerment frameworks.

Ethics

The ethics framework is the dominant paradigm in social science research; all researchers are expected to take into account the ethical issues raised by their research. This concern manifests itself in ethics committees and guide-lines like the ones formulated by the TESOL committee mentioned earlier. However, the nature and limits of respon-sibility are generally narrowly confined to getting as much information as possible from the researched while not ex-ploiting or abusing them, and without violating their pri-vacy or breaching confidentiality. In other words, you are expected to be nice and interfere as little as possible in your subjects' lives. Do not bore and do not hurt anyone, but get what you want.

Sometimes, however, a research design requires that the researcher conceal her real interests, and perhaps use small deceptions to deal with the classic "observer's paradox." As Cameron et al. (1993) pointed out, the decision as to what constitutes an appropriate "innocuous deception" lies with the researcher, and herein lies the root of the asymmetrical relationship between researcher and researched, that is, the researcher is the active legitimate, knowledge seeker and the researched is the passive repository of the knowl-edge.

In essence, the ethics framework is one of research on subjects. Of course, the subjects are entitled to certain ethi-cal protections, but the researcher decides the extent of those considerations by setting the research agenda. More often than not, those researched are not brought into the picture until the research agenda has been carefully delin-eated. The origin of this framework is in the scientific method and centers on the issue of where truth comes from. In this positivist approach, there exists both a culture and uninvolved scientists who do science, that is, getting at the one truth. It is not important nor is it even a goal that such research have any positive effect on the subjects. If it does, it is a bonus; if it does not, as Cameron et al. put it, "so long as no actual harm is done, it can still be accepted as ethical" (p. 83). In effect, this framework does not say much about the context or the people who are being researched. The main concern is for the researcher's relationship with academia: avoid someone else's territory, do not fudge, and acknowledge your sources. It is a starting point.

Advocacy

The second framework Cameron et al. discussed is the advocacy framework. This framework evolves out of a desire not simply to avoid harming subjects, but from a more positive inclination to help them. This inclination may be operationalized as part of the design of a research program, or may develop later in the process of interacting with the community as a result of needs identified by the researcher or as a result of a petition from the community. Thus, this becomes research on and for them, because it places the researcher in the role of advocate. A well-known example of work within this framework is Labov's role in the Ann Arbor lawsuit regarding the place of American Vernacular Black English (AVBE) in the public schools. He subsequently wrote a paper (Labov, 1982) in which he laid down certain principles of objectivity and commitment for researchers, arguing that advocacy is not just a bonus or an optional extra, but under certain circumstances constitutes an obligation. He proposed "the principle of the debt incurred." In other words, if a community assists a researcher by providing access and information, researchers incur a debt and are bound to use their knowledge and expertise to assist the community.

It is important from the perspective of science to note that Labov took issue with the notion that commitment necessarily threatens a researcher's objectivity—a fundamental of a positivist philosophy of science—arguing that the responsibility for accurately and fairly representing a community could sharpen a researcher's commitment and presentation of the facts, thus pressuring researchers to seek the truth more doggedly.

However, Cameron et al. (1993) pointed out that although it is important for experts to act as advocates, it is perhaps more important for the individuals in question to gain the knowledge and skills to act for themselves. They believe that although it is extreme to suggest that everyone can become an expert, if only the expert advocate has access to specialist knowledge, that expert has access to significant power because he may be the only one who has all the information needed for good decision-making. Thus, the decision-making process may be out of the hands of those who will be the most affected. For example, although the Ann Arbor community agreed on a course of action, it is not at all clear that this was a decision shared by any other AVBE community in the United States. Nevertheless, it is entirely possible that a solution found for one group may be applied to another in the name of efficiency or coherent policy. Communities encapsulate diverse interests, and if members of those other communities do not possess the expert information they need to carry on internal debate, there is a clear danger that outside advocates (i.e., those specialists with experience in other communities or contexts) will end up making choices for them.

Cameron et al. further argued that the requirements of a positivist approach lead "almost inevitably to the objectification of informants by researchers" (p. 86). They went on to claim that "if...people are not objects and should not be treated like objects, this surely entitles them to more than just respectful (ethical) treatment" (p. 86). The implication of such an approach is that the researcher and the researched must interact and that "researchers should not try to pretend that their subjects can be studied as if the former were outside the social universe that included the latter" (p. 86).[1]

Critics of positivism have argued that a researcher who observes a certain human behavior should not only be interested in describing what the individual appears to be

---

[1] The danger for science of treating subjects at arm's length was made clear recently by a student in a seminar on ethics in linguistics fieldwork at the University of Oregon. She pointed out how in her Native American group a particular famous linguist was not favorably viewed, and, hence, the members of the community regularly engaged in giving him "bad" data.

doing, but what the individual thinks she is doing, which can become known only through interaction between the observer and the observed. For example, the teacher in the situation I described earlier wanted to be portrayed as a person who behaved in a certain way (the right way), and who could get her students to behave in a certain way (produce the second language). This was how she negotiated her persona; it was how she wished to be viewed. Such performance data should not be considered contaminated (i.e., atypical), but rather as a reflection of how she construed good teaching, and a reflection of what she has found to be successful pedagogy with her students.

Empowerment

If we are persuaded that it is useless and counterproductive to insist on objectification of our subjects, then we need to consider the possibility of doing research not only on or for certain groups, but also with them. This is the third framework, the one which Cameron et al. (1993), called an empowerment or collaborative framework. Briefly, in this paradigm there is no culture or classroom out there; there is no uninvolved scientist. You are part of it and it develops with you.

This framework recognizes that power is not a monolithic or static entity. The relationship between researcher and researched is more complex than simply a powerful or oppressive "us" versus a powerless passive "them." As Becker (1993) pointed out, "Uncoerced subjects are typically as successful as researchers in carrying out their agendas and, where necessary, in concealing them or out-maneuvering them" (p. 95). The teacher I discussed earlier was taking full advantage of her superior knowledge to even the playing field, and at least at that point in our relationship, I was the less powerful. Thus, I am convinced that a value in this framework is its explicit recognition that power is "shifting and variable rather than static" (Cameron et al., 1993, p. 90). We, as researchers, are not in a position to confer it or to empower others, but we can foster a web of reciprocity in which we mutually work toward goals we have defined in part through collaboration.

Hence, in an empowerment framework, what those you study want to know becomes an issue and the researcher should take such needs into account. This does not imply, however, that the main or only criterion for valid research is immediately perceived utility to the researched. It is possible that what a researcher predicted the researched would not find interesting may turn out to be exactly what they do find interesting. As Cameron et al. pointed out, much of what social scientists produce as research is already known by those they study, and researchers' essential utility is that they create a synthesis of information. They present such information in a broader context, and it is in this form that the researched may learn something about themselves that they might not have consciously known before. This is what makes knowledge valuable and something we should share.

Positivist ethical research precludes such exchange of information, but surely none of us would suggest that we not share what we find out in our research with teachers. Our responsibility lies more in sharing it in a way that is effective. Harries-Jones (1985) suggested that what too often happens is that we engage in the educator's equivalent of the economist's theory of "trickle-down development." Educational trickledown runs somewhat like this: throw capital in the form of education at the elite, and the diffusion of ideas will bring about ripples of adjustment as they flow outward and downward to the bottom of the development pool. In the case of applied linguistics, he would claim that we throw our research capital at each other in conferences, proceedings, and publication, and maybe assume that the ideas that we toss about will somehow, someday have an effect on what other people do in the classroom. Hence, as with economic trickledown, those who are most in need are the least well-served, because often the information they need is not available to them or not available in a form they can use.

Alternatives in Action

Having done things "wrong" seems to imply that there is a way to do things "right," but I am not sure this is really possible. It is clear that a researcher should spend time getting to know the students, teachers, and issues of the research site well before implementing a research program involving the cooperation of school personnel. Establishing such a relationship smooths over some of the rockier places encountered when two activities are at cross-purposes, namely, teaching and research on teaching. It is not at all guaranteed that having a friendly relationship with school personnel will eliminate interpersonal disagreement. Even close families have disputes, and the ability to have a dialogue about dissatisfactions might even be what makes some families stronger. It pushes them to express their needs more clearly.

It is also clear that researchers need to figure out a means of contributing to the classrooms they study, that is, do something useful for the community. This could be in the form of information and research findings, but it might also be in a less tangible form like providing the moral support a teacher needs to carry on from day to day, interacting in a positive and interested way with the students, or just providing a springboard for ideas or outside validation of a difficult job well done. It is the researcher's responsibility to find the most appropriate way to provide a positive force in the school environment.

It is also clear that sometimes the projects that we conceptualize are not interesting or pertinent to the teachers' perceived needs at that moment. I would certainly not suggest that such research be abandoned. Needs can change; perceptions evolve. Having a long-term relationship with a classroom or school entails being part of the change and evolution. It also means that research becomes a research program, not simply a one-shot deal.

CONCLUSION

This chapter suggests that as classroom-based researchers we can better function in our research sites if we see ourselves as potentially unwelcome, unimportant, or unnecessary visitors to another society about to engage in a significant cross-cultural experience. This view will help us contextualize what we might otherwise feel is uncooperative, inflexible, or obstructionist behavior on the part of those we are studying or those we believe we are trying to help. If we see ourselves as visitors, we can better understand why those we research might see us as demanding, intrusive, dogmatic, and boring guests who come too often and stay too long.

As fieldworkers, I believe it is important for us to balance the needs of academia with the needs of the people. Working in a classroom will surely change the composition of that community. Just as in anthropological fieldwork, we classroom-based researchers essentially become one more mouth to feed, a source of fear, a big spender or provider, a source of amusement, self-doubt, change, or disruption in routine. We certainly have a responsibility to study and research second language classrooms systematically in order to expand our understanding of learning and teaching. In pursuing this goal, I think we also need to ask whether it is enough simply to be ethical or whether we should include empowerment or collaboration as part of our responsibility. But, it may be that we will ultimately have no choice.

REFERENCES

Becker, L. C. (1993). Commentary: Subjects are not patients. *Language & Communication, 13*, 96–96.

Cameron, D., Frazer, E., Harvey, P., Rampton, B., & Richardson, K. (1993). Ethics, advocacy and empowerment: Issues of method in researching language. *Language & Communication, 13*, 81–94.

Goffman, E. (1961). *Asylums*. Garden City, NJ: Doubleday.

Harries-Jones, P. (1985). From cultural translator to advocate: Changing circles of interpretation. In R. Paine (Ed.), *Advocacy and anthropology, first encounters* (pp. 224–248). St. John's, Newfoundland: Institute of Social and Economic Research, Memorial University of Newfoundland.

Labov, W. (1982). Objectivity and commitment in linguistic science: The case of the Black English trial in Ann Arbor. *Language in Society, 11*, 165–201.

Tarone, E. (1980). TESOL Research Committee Report: Guidelines for ethical research in ESL. *TESOL Quarterly, 14*, 383–388.

Chapter 4

Issues and Problems
in Reporting Classroom Research

Charlene G. Polio
Michigan State University

Any classroom research presents difficulties, but those difficulties and the stages that prove to be most problematic may be related to the research paradigms within which one is working. Because applied linguistics is an interdisciplinary field, the research paradigms have been varied, with even the subset of second language classroom research spanning a range of research types. Furthermore, classroom research has also drawn simultaneously from several paradigms, often making it difficult to classify, especially as many researchers do not explicitly state their paradigm. In this chapter, different types of classroom research are discussed in order to address the points at which the various types of research encounter different problems.

One of the most comprehensive discussions of research paradigms with reference to second language education is Lynch (1996). Although he focuses specifically on program evaluation, some of his distinctions and comments are useful in classifying second language classroom research in general. He, like others, describes some research as falling into the rationalistic, quantitative paradigm; here he includes true experiments and quasiexperiments. These pose logistical problems to be reconciled at the planning stages, including whether all the variables can be controlled for, whether random sampling can be obtained, and whether teachers and administrators will agree to implement the design. (See Kuiper and Plough, this volume, for a discussion of this last issue.) Assuming the logistical problems are overcome in that the teachers agree to implement a treatment and do indeed follow instructions, writing up the research is relatively straightforward: The treatment either worked or did not work. If it is concluded that the treatment should have included x, y, or z, the problems with the treatment can be attributed to the research design.

Nonexperimental classroom research is generally classified as naturalistic, qualitative research. Lynch (1996) says of this kind of research that "the emphasis is on observing, describing, interpreting, and understanding how events take place in the real world rather than in a controlled laboratory-like setting" (p. 14).

Research that falls into the naturalistic paradigm subscribes to a different world view than research in a rationalistic, quantitative paradigm, which holds that truth is objective. The naturalistic paradigms contend that there are multiple realities and that truth is not objective and observable. Lynch makes the important point that paradigm does not dictate method; although naturalistic research tends to be qualitative, the researcher may classify and quantify various phenomena.

Herein, the focus of this chapter is on research that is not experimental; that is, research that describes what is currently taking place (e.g., ethnographic research), as opposed to research that attempts to manipulate variables. This does not mean that all nonexperimental research falls into a naturalistic paradigm; some of it seems to assume the positivistic view of the world that there is an objective truth. Thus, the kinds of research will be classified by method instead of by world view.

Nonexperimental research poses a different set of problems from experimental research. It is intrusive but in a different way from experimental research. Whereas one specifically does not ask participants to change their behavior to accommodate the researcher, and indeed hopes they do not, the researcher is present, watching, and probing. The first problem is to find a teacher to agree to participate. Because teachers are expected to go about their daily routines, reluctance on their part is not related to the fact that they have been asked to accommodate the researcher by doing assigned tasks in class or by committing any extra time to the project. Instead, they may be concerned about either implicit or explicit evaluation by the researcher. And such fears, as will be shown later, may not be unfounded.

Assuming that one has found a willing teacher who gives informed consent, whether that participation is minimal (e.g., videotaping the classroom for one lesson) or extensive (e.g., a semester-long ethnographic study), there are further difficulties. If one hopes to tell others about the findings and thereby contribute to the knowledge of the field, one must write up and publish the research. At this point, an important question is: How can one write about research conducted in the classroom without offending the sensibilities of the teachers involved? Despite informed consent and promises of anonymity, teachers will no doubt be able to recognize themselves. Supervisors giving consent or colleagues aware of the research may also be able to identify, or at least narrow down, the teacher being described.

These problems related to writing about teachers within the context of general classroom research are presented with regard to different types of published nonexperimental classroom research. Then, specific examples from two studies of foreign language (FL) classrooms (Duff & Polio, 1990; Polio & Duff, 1994) are presented. The purpose of the first study was to quantify the amount of target language (TL) that teachers used in university FL classes; the purpose of the second was to examine the functions for which the teachers used the students' native language (L1) and TL in such classes. The chapter ends with suggestions for second language classroom research, several of which were incorporated into these two studies; these suggestions may help minimize some of the problems that arise in publicly disseminating nonexperimental classroom research.

ASSUMPTIONS

Before continuing, I would like to put forth three assumptions. The first is that examining the language classroom is essential to the field of second and foreign language teaching. Long (1980), in his now classic "black box" article, argued that what goes on in the classroom and the teacher's role in the classroom, may be the most important factors in second language acquisition in an instructed context.[1] Long (1984) extended this argument to program evaluation research saying classroom (process) research must be done in conjunction with outcomes (product) research. Beretta (1986) argued that what goes on in a laboratory setting may have little relationship to what goes on in a real classroom; in other words, results from a laboratory experiment cannot necessarily be generalized to the classroom.

The second assumption is that everyone goes into classroom research with values and a point of view about what should or should not be done in the classroom. These views may be based on previous research in the field, or on one's personal experience. Yet, how each researcher deals with these implicit or explicit values varies considerably.

And third, while pains should be taken to represent the teacher's point of view, especially because no teacher teaches under ideal conditions, we cannot assume that everything that the teacher does is correct. What we can do is try to find out why the teachers teach the way they do. Furthermore, reporting, discussing, and critiquing teaching behaviors will benefit others, including preservice teachers, other teachers, and most importantly, one would hope, the students.

PROBLEMS

To point out specific problems in writing up nonexperimental research, examples are given from three (not mutually exclusive) kinds of research that may involve examining the

---

[1] This is not to say that what goes on outside the classroom is unimportant, especially with regard to the learning of reading and writing where students may do much work on their own. (I thank Patricia Duff for this observation.)

language classroom; ethnography, program evaluation, and what I will call nonethnographic, nonexperimental research.

Ethnography

With regard to ethnographic research, Watso-Gegeo (1988) wrote, with specific reference to ESL classrooms, that theory is important to help the researcher decide what to focus on, bearing in mind that the description is still holistic and must take into account the entire system. One example of ethnographic research in a second language setting is found in Crago (1992), who looked at classroom interaction in an Inuit setting in Canada. In one example she quoted a teacher as saying:

> These little white kids, even if they are learning in a second language, they talk circles around the Inuit kids. The Inuit kids just sit there looking at me with big eyes, saying nothing. I hate to admit it, but one day I just couldn't stand their silence any longer, I ended up shaking this Inuk boy and screaming, "Talk to me for heaven's sake." (p. 497)

Taken out of context, this account might make the teacher seem insensitive. Yet, when one reads Crago's study and sees the reasons for the teacher's comments (differences in language socialization and interaction patterns), one can understand the frustration on both sides and, it is hoped, does not judge. The point is that because ethnographic research clearly attempts to represent multiple perspectives, the problems of offending the teacher's sensibilities are diminished; the teacher's view is always addressed as it is part of the entire system.

Program Evaluation

Program evaluation is one type of research that can be either or both quantitative and qualitative and that may fall into a rationalistic or naturalistic paradigm; program evaluation is a kind of research related to a specific purpose as opposed to a specific paradigm. Brown (1989) defined evaluation as, "the systematic collection and analysis of all relevant information necessary to promote the improvement of a curriculum, and assess its effectiveness and efficiency, as well as the participants' attitudes within the context of the particular institutions involved" (p. 223).

Program evaluation research is addressed here because it often involves classroom research, and is, by definition, evaluative. An evaluation of a second language program is often undertaken initially for a specific audience (funding agency, institution); yet eventually, the author(s) will want to publish the results of the work. Here again there arises the problem of writing up such work without offending or even harming those involved. Below are three examples of problematic findings.

The first was noted in work of my own (as cited in Brinton, Snow, & Wesche, 1989) which evaluated an interinstitutional program in China, "...the Chinese teachers reported spending many additional hours on lesson planning since they felt less confident or unprepared to cope linguistically, and as such did not participate as fully in lesson planning and materials development as had been envisioned in the original plan" (p. 80). Lynch (1992) described the evaluation of an interinstitutional U.S.–Mexican project, "After reviewing the relevant data in the journals and other sources such as the Daily Log and Meeting notes, it seems clear that there were major personality problems on the Project which adversely affected its development" (p. 87). Beretta (1992) reported on his evaluation of the Bangalore project in India, "It was already known from observers' reports (Davies, 1983; Brumfit, 1984) that the regular teacher reverted to form-focused teaching, so the interest here was in the non-regular teachers" (pp. 255–256).

In one sense, we can explain all of the above situations. In the Chinese context, the teachers were being forced to do something for which they were not prepared. Lynch went on to talk about why such difficulties occurred and the fact that the problems could easily occur in any context abroad. Beretta acknowledged that the teachers he referred to were teaching out of a concern for the students. Yet seen another way, the Chinese teachers were linguistically unprepared, the teachers in Mexico had difficulty working together, and those in India were not following instructions. Such unintended interpretations are possible on the part of any participants in any of the programs.

The fact is that little is said about writing up program evaluation research which examines teachers and the classroom. One book on reporting results of program evaluation (Morris, Fitz-Gibbon, & Freeman, 1987) said only that all evaluation findings are political and that an evaluator should not evaluate a specific individual. Yet, the above examples show that one may still end up criticizing teachers as a group.

Lynch (1996) touched upon this issue in his discussion of reporting findings. He mentioned the importance of the sociopolitical climate in which the program is situated, and also, the focus here, the problem of offending those involved. He stated:

> If the evaluator and/or audiences are committed to a par-
> ticular course of action based on the findings of the evalua-
> tion, it may be necessary to translate results into language
> that does not offend the sensibilities of teachers, students,
> administrators, or the community within which the program
> is situated. (p. 175)

Nonethnographic, Nonexperimental Research

The final type of research, and potentially the most problematic, is what is called here nonethnographic, nonexperimental research. This is where one goes into pre-existing classrooms, and as in carrying out ethnographic studies, does not attempt to manipulate any variables. Unlike ethnographic studies, however, the researcher focuses on only one feature of the classroom. The researcher often asks a specific question that will result in an implicit evaluation of teaching practices, in relation to findings of previous research. This kind of research is also different from program evaluation in that in program evaluation, all involved parties know that evaluation is the ultimate purpose of any classroom observation.

In Duff and Polio (1990), the research questions were:

1. What is the ratio of English use to L2 use by teachers in FL classrooms?
2. What factors are related to the use of English and the L2?

3. What are teachers' and students' perceptions and attitudes regarding the use of English in the FL classroom? (p.154)

These questions were not asked without reason. The study began by citing previous literature in support of maximal use of the target language. We wanted to examine what was actually happening in foreign language classrooms and why. The following excerpt indicates how the research was approached:

> Certain variables were considered for their possible influence on the language of the classroom. As this study is conducted within the qualitative paradigm, we are not attempting to show causal relationships among the variables. Rather, these variables guided us in the preparation of questionnaires and interviews and were helpful in interpreting some of the results. (Duff & Polio, 1990, p. 155)

The variables under consideration (e.g., departmental policy, teachers' perception of L1/TL distance) could be neither quantified nor manipulated, thus ruling out experimental research. The overriding paradigm may be considered positivistic if one considers the following statement in Polio and Duff (1994):

> Through an examination of a variety of university FL classrooms and characterization of the teachers' uses of the TL and English, this study addresses a basic question: When do teachers tend to use English, rather than the TL, and for what functions? While we cannot directly address the difficult but important issue of the actual effects of a particular ratio of English/TL usage on acquisition, we feel that baseline studies such as ours which describe FL teachers' classroom language and discuss the possible constraints posed by this linguistic interaction prepare the way for future applied work in this area employing experimental research methods. (p. 314)

There is some sense here that the qualitative research can precede or lead to experimental research, a view discussed by Crookes (1991). The reporting of the research becomes problematic because one does not approach the research

with the same questions with which one approaches ethnographic research, although ethnographic research on a
smaller set of classes is also suggested as a possible follow-
up study to Polio and Duff (1994). On one hand, teachers'
attitudes and perceptions were an important issue, as stated
in the initial research questions; on the other hand, previous research pointed to, but did not necessarily prove the
effects of, maximal use of the TL.

Before discussing some of the difficulties faced in describing the teachers from our studies, examples are given from
two other studies in this category which exhibit similar dilemmas. As in the Duff and Polio studies, both of these
studies, one older and one more recent, examined speech
addressed to second language learners by teachers.

Schinke-Llano (1983) found that Limited English Proficiency (LEP) children were spoken to differently than non-
LEP students. In content classes, they were interacted with
less frequently and the interaction tended to be managerial
rather than instructional. She concluded, "As a result of
these characteristics, LEP students in content classes experience a difference [sic] linguistic environment than their
non-LEP counterparts. Such a differential treatment may
have consequences for self-esteem, second language acquisition, and mastery of content subjects" (p. 160).

Schinke-Llano was appropriately cautious in her conclusions emphasizing that the effects of such interactions are
not certain. Furthermore, she did attempt possible explanations for the teachers' language use, such as the teachers do not call on the LEP students so as to avoid embar-
rassing them. Nevertheless, teachers or administrators reading about their own classrooms might feel as though they
either were depriving these students, or they needed a
chance to defend their teaching behaviors. The point is that
the researcher began the research with some sense of effective classroom interactional patterns.

Another study that looks at classroom interaction is
Weissberg (1994). He examined ESL writing classes citing
previous research that has contended that certain discourse
patterns are important to writing. Specifically, he claimed
that having teachers and students collaboratively explore
topics to be written about is important to successful writ-

ing. He found, though, that discourse moves related to such collaboration are the least frequent types of discourse patterns in the classes he examined, and concluded that teachers may need to be made more aware of discourse patterns that fall into this category. Although he provided very specific and helpful suggestions, it is still the case that the teachers who participated in the research were being described as doing something less than optimal to promote student writing.

Let us return now to some comments from Duff and Polio (1990), and Polio and Duff (1994). In Duff and Polio, we claimed that prior research pointed to the importance of maximal use of the TL. Although an extreme case, we pointed out one teacher in the study who used the TL in only 10% of his utterances and said in his interview that he used it about 45% of the time. Furthermore, another teacher who taught a linguistically related language used the TL in 94% of his utterances. We ended the study, as did Weissberg, with specific suggestions for teachers to help them change their discourse patterns.

Polio and Duff (1994) also pointed out some problematic teacher language use giving specific excerpts, thus increasing the likelihood that the teacher may have recognized him or herself. We gave an example of a teacher reminding students of the departmental policy to speak only the TL, but then switching to English herself a few turns later. Furthermore, commenting on the findings that teachers tended to use English for classroom academic vocabulary, we stated:

> It is somewhat paradoxical, however, that teachers use English for vocabulary of this type. Such expressions tend to be high in frequency in an academic setting and are often very predictable. Thus, they should be very easy for students to learn. The Korean teacher, for example, suggested that her students did indeed know these words in the TL, yet she used English. By not hearing these words in the TL, the students first lose the opportunity to infer the meaning of the vocabulary item from context and to process this information in the TL. In addition, if a student does not understand exactly what the teacher is saying in the TL and believes that it may be important, there is greater likelihood that the student will ask for clarification and that genuine communication will result. (p. 321)

For almost every use of English in the FL classrooms found, we presented a similar discussion of why it might be better to use the TL.

In all of this research, efforts were made so that an outsider could not identify the teacher, yet in many cases, the teachers could probably identify themselves. This is problematic because often in these types of studies, recommendations for helping teachers to change their behaviors are given, thus implying negative qualities in their teaching. As stated earlier, one assumption is that such studies will help in future efforts for teacher development. These studies were, in fact, funded by the Office of Instructional Development at the institution at which they were conducted. The results of these studies have been used to promote discussions in workshops for foreign language teaching assistants and in TESOL methodology classes. How then can one report on teaching behaviors as part of qualitative research or program evaluation?

SUGGESTIONS

Below is a list of suggestions to help minimize some of the problems encountered in writing up classroom research.

Acknowledge the Teacher's Point of View

Presenting all points of view is essential in ethnographic research, however, it may not be done in other nonexperimental research. Through interviews, we tried to get at the teachers' beliefs and attitudes about what they were doing. In some cases, the teachers' comments helped us to understand some of the behavior that conflicted with assumptions about language learning in the literature. For example, in many cases, we found that teachers spoke more English out of a concern for their students. Consider two excerpts from Polio and Duff (1994):

> I always- when we are talking about grammar that is always in English because they are not able to understand [Slavic] on this level. They just started to learn [Slavic] so there is no purpose to learn- to teach them- to teach them grammar

using [Slavic]. They will not understand any word. (p. 317)

Clearly, the teacher was concerned about her students learning the material. She also said in her interview that she had
had to learn English completely in English and that this
had been very stressful for her. She apparently did not want
her students to have the same difficulty. Another teacher
explained that the students had to learn the grammar to
pass a departmental exam. If he had spent time explaining
the grammar in the TL, it would have taken longer and not
as much material would have been covered.

Yet another teacher stated in Polio and Duff (1994):

> The first quarter I - I did speak a lot of - probably too much
> English in class. And for two reasons. First, first of all be-
> cause they don't know that much German and secondly if
> you want to create some kind of relaxed atmosphere I think
> it's a hard thing to do in German only.... If I talk English I
> have the feeling that everybody immediately gets everything
> which makes me feel fine. If I talk German I feel better in
> terms of language but I know I have to be very careful and
> probably repeat things and make it easier. (pp. 323–324)

Representing the teachers' point of view shows us that they
want their students to learn; they do not want to put too
much pressure on them; they want them to pass the exams; and they want to make learning pleasant. This helps
counter other possible perspectives such as that teachers
do not know techniques for teaching grammar in the TL;
they do not feel that their students need to learn quickly;
and they care only about their students passing exams, not
learning the language.

Acknowledge the Realities of the Teaching Context

All teachers teach under constraints of time, materials and
syllabi, and student and supervisor expectations. This is
related to the above comments in that the teachers may
often discuss the constraints they are under. One of our
attempts to acknowledge such constraints is the following
comment:

These suggestions [on how to use more of the TL] are meant to help teachers modify their language use, given the curricular priorities that have already been established (e.g., for a grammar-based syllabus). Reexamining those priorities might also be a worthwhile process. Another approach to expanding opportunities for TL exposure and practice would, of course, entail modifying methodologies, material, and curricula which tend to preclude greater use of the foreign language in these FL classrooms (e.g., by trying to cover too much material in too short a time). (p. 322)

Based on the teachers' comments, we attempted to acknowledge constraints the teachers were under, such as having to cover a certain amount of material. One suggestion was to modify the curriculum to help the teachers deal with such constraints. On the positive side, such studies may be an impetus for change. It may, however, be difficult to relate such constraints in the research if teachers are reluctant to discuss them. For example, all the teachers in our study were native speakers of the TL and thus were not asked about their language proficiency. But, if this study had been conducted with teachers who were not native speakers of the TL, it is easy to imagine a situation where the issue of their language proficiency might arise. Teachers might then be afraid to admit to a lack of proficiency to teach in the TL because of embarrassment, or because they were being forced to teach a language they were not prepared to teach. Such situations must be viewed sensitively.

Reveal as Little Information About Teachers as Necessary

One is often tempted, and understandably so, in discussing classroom research, to fully describe the setting and participants. This must be balanced, of course, with protecting the anonymity of the teachers. In Duff and Polio (1990), we listed the 13 languages without identifying them. Not including the languages detracted from the study in that one of the factors potentially related to teachers' language use was the typology of the language and its perceived distance from English. Even though such information would not have allowed one to identify teachers personally, in many cases it could have narrowed the possible participants. Instead of identifying the languages, we made comments about which languages were linguistically related and which had different writing systems, for example.

In the second study, it became apparent that in order to provide excerpts from the classes, the languages had to be revealed. We chose 6 of the 13 classes for an analysis of the teachers' language use of English and the TL. At this point, we did not reveal the languages of the other 7 classes. In one of the 6 classes, we stated only the language family because there had only been one teacher of that particular language at the time the study was done. This forced us to delete actual TL words in the classroom excerpts. Further-more, it would have been interesting to describe the teach-ers' backgrounds and experience in more detail, but this would have compromised their anonymity.

Debrief Teachers on the Research

When a researcher gets consent from teachers to observe or record their classrooms, only a certain amount about the purpose of the study can be revealed so as not to affect a teacher's behavior. However, after the study is done, a researcher has an obligation to provide the teacher with details of the study. The first step in doing this took place after the interview with the teachers. We explained to the teachers that we were examining English and TL use in the classroom. Some teachers showed little interest in hearing this; others opened up and explained in further detail why they used the two languages the way they did. This was helpful in that it provided us with another chance, after the interview, to hear the teachers' points of view on the issue we were examining.

The second step was to send the teachers a note thank-ing them and offering them copies of our initial (prepublication) report. This seemed preferable to simply sending the report which may have been perceived as un-solicited advice. One step which perhaps could have been taken, was to ask the teachers for feedback. It may be that after reading about the research, the teachers could have provided additional insights.

Take Teaching Suggestions from Teachers

At the end of our first study, we offered suggestions for increasing TL use in the classroom. We had observed one, in our opinion, very skilled teacher, who spoke English the last 5 minutes of class. This provided the students with an opportunity to ask questions and clarify earlier comments made in the TL. Although we were critical of other uses of the students' native language, this one struck us as helpful; the students and teacher knew they would have the end of class to clarify problems and thus did not speak a word of English prior to that point.

An approach related to the above comments would be to single out particularly skilled teachers for study. Cumming (1992) took such an approach in looking at the instructional routines of ESL composition teachers. He chose teachers by asking the coordinator of a university ESL program to nominate instructors who possessed expertise in the area of composition teaching. This allows one to report on teaching behaviors in a positive way, and findings can then be disseminated to other pre- or inservice teachers who may benefit.

Acknowledge Personal Perspective

At one point, ethnographic research assumed a fieldworker entered the field without preconceived notions about what might be found. This idea no longer holds in mainstream ethnographic research. As Denizen and Lincoln (1994) stated, "Any gaze is always filtered through the lenses of language, gender, social class, race, and ethnicity. There are no observations, only observations socially situated in the worlds of the observer and the observed" (p. 12).

Other types of research, such as some of the nonethnographic research discussed here, rarely acknowledge a personal perspective. In our study, the perspective, in fact, was a bit unusual because our perspective was actually that of a student. We were taking an FL class together and felt constant frustration that the teacher was speaking in English most of the time.[2] We were not able to understand why a teacher would do this and thus set out to investigate. Our perspective when the study began, came from two viewpoints: as graduate students in applied linguistics aware of language teaching research, and as ESL/EFL teachers, with several years experience between us, who conducted all of our English classes in English in a variety of contexts and over a range of levels.

When we approached the teachers, 11 of whom were graduate student teaching assistants, we were peers, that is, fellow graduate students. When we wrote up the research, we became researchers, an arguably more powerful position. One could say that the power relationship between our research subjects, the teachers, was changing from student to peer to researcher.

Use Stimulus Recall Techniques

Another way to elicit teachers' perspectives on their behavior in the classroom is to use a technique like stimulus recall. This technique involves having the teacher watch a videotape of his or her teaching with the researcher. Either teacher or the researcher may stop the tape and discuss decisions that the teacher made at certain points. Such a technique was used by Johnson (1992) who examined preservice ESL teachers. Her study was more exploratory, in that the research questions were general and did not focus on a specific issue. Yet this technique could have been used in the various studies mentioned here to help the researcher further explore certain teaching behaviors. We did not employ this technique in our studies, but suggested it

---

[2]After observing each of the 13 classes, we gave the students, mostly undergraduates, a questionnaire. One of the questions was: How much English would you like your teacher to use in class? Among the choices, "more than now," "the same as now," or "less than now," between 72% and 100% of the students in each class said, "the same as now." This seemed to have no relationship to the amount of English/TL being used by their teacher. These students obviously did not share our perspective.

as another way to explore L1/L2 language choice.

CONCLUSION

Much has been written recently on the relationship between research, theory, published articles, and teachers, most notably, Pennycook (1989) and Clarke (1994). Both are critical of a system in which published academics dictate teaching practices when the writers of such articles are rarely language teachers themselves. Given the above discussion of the ways in which teachers can be portrayed in classroom research, such criticisms are not completely unfounded. Clarke went a step further arguing:

> Research reports and theoretical speculation, even those which focus on classroom issues, are limited in depth and detail. No matter how diligently researchers work to include all the variables that teachers deal with in a typical day, the data they collect and the conclusions they draw are, by necessity, less complex than the reality that teachers confront every day. Such speculation is, therefore, reductionist and inaccurate. (p. 16)

Is there any value then of a researcher doing classroom research that attempts to focus on one particular question? I stated earlier that one assumption of this chapter was that reporting, discussing, and critiquing teaching behaviors can be beneficial to pre- and inservice teachers and ultimately, to students. I hope that those who do research on language teaching will continue a discussion of how best to approach and report classroom research, as opposed to abandoning it, so as to better consider the sensibilities of all involved.

ACKNOWLEDGMENTS

I would like to thank Brian Lynch and Patricia Duff for their comments on an earlier version of this chapter. Needless to say, they do not necessarily agree with all of the views presented here.

REFERENCES

Beretta, A. (1986). Toward a methodology of ESL program evaluation. *TESOL Quarterly, 29,* 144–155.

Beretta, A. (1992). What can be learned from the Bangalore Evaluation. In J. C. Alderson & A. Beretta (Eds.), *Evaluating second language education* (pp. 250–271). Cambridge, England: Cambridge University Press.

Brinton, D., Snow, M., & Wesche, M. (1989). *Content-based second language instruction.* New York: Newbury House.

Brown, J. D. (1989). Language program evaluation: A synthesis of existing possibilities. In R. K. Johnson (Ed.), *The second language curriculum* (pp. 222–241). Cambridge, England: Cambridge University Press.

Brumfit, C. J. (1984). The Bangalore procedural syllabus. *English Language Teaching Journal, 38,* 233–241.

Clarke, M. (1994). The dysfunctions of the theory/practice discourse. *TESOL Quarterly, 28,* 9– 26.

Crago, M. (1992). Communicative interaction and second language acquisition: An Inuit example. *TESOL Quarterly, 26,* 487–505.

Crookes, G. (1991). Second language speech production: A methodologically-oriented overview. *Studies in Second Language Acquisition, 13,* 113–132.

Cumming, A. (1992). Instructional routines in ESL composition teaching: A case study of three teachers. *Journal of Second Language Writing, 1,* 17–36.

Davies, A. (1983). *Evaluation and the Bangalore/Madras Communicational Teaching Project.* Unpublished manuscript, University of Edinburgh, Department of Applied Linguistics.

Denizen, N., & Lincoln, Y. (Eds.). (1994). Introduction: Entering the field of qualitative research. *Handbook of qualitative research* (pp. 1–17). Thousand Oaks, CA: Sage.

Duff, P., & Polio, C. (1990). How much foreign language is there in the foreign language classroom? *Modern Language Journal, 74,* 154–166.

Johnson, K. (1992). Learning to teach: Instructional actions and decisions of preservice ESL teachers. *TESOL Quarterly, 26,* 507–536.

Long, M. H. (1980). Inside the "black box": Methodological issues in classroom research on language learning. *Language Learning, 30,* 1–42.

Long, M. H. (1994). Process and product in ESL program evaluation. *TESOL Quarterly, 18,* 409–425.

Lynch, B. (1992). Evaluating a program inside and out. In J. C. Alderson & A. Beretta (Eds.), *Evaluating second language education* (pp. 61–96). Cambridge, England: Cambridge University Press.

Lynch, B. (1996). *Language program evaluation: Theory and practice.* Cambridge, England: Cambridge University Press.

Morris, L., Fitz-Gibbon, C., & Freeman, M. (1987). *How to communicate evaluation findings.* Newbury Park, CA: Sage.

Pennycook, A. (1989). The concept of method, interested knowledge, and the politics of language teaching. *TESOL Quarterly, 23,* 589–618.

Polio, C., & Duff, P. (1994). Teachers' language use in university foreign language classrooms: A qualitative analysis of English and target language alternation. *Modern Language Journal, 78,* 313–326.

Schinke-Llano, L. (1983). Foreigner talk in content classrooms. In H. Seliger & M. Long (Eds.), *Classroom oriented research in second language acquisition* (pp. 146–165). Rowley, MA: Newbury House.

Watson-Gegeo, K. (1988). Ethnography in ESL: Defining the essentials. *TESOL Quarterly, 22,* 575–592.

Weissberg, B. (1994). Speaking of writing: Some functions of talk in the ESL composition class. *Journal of Second Language Writing, 3,* 121–140.

Chapter 5

Classroom-Based Research as a Collaborative Effort

Lawrence Kuiper
Indiana University
India Plough
East Lansing Public Schools

In this chapter, we suggest a collegial approach to classroom-based research which may alleviate many of the problems often assumed inherent to such research whether it be qualitative, quantitative, or a combination of the two. Although unforeseen obstacles inevitably arise in the course of research, many of the difficulties often associated with large institutions may be avoided or at least diminished. After providing a general overview of a specific research project, this chapter examines not only the aspects that complicated its implementation, but also those that made it run smoothly. We suggest that an understanding of the sociology of a major institution and its communication networks (see Markee, this volume) is at the core of the successful completion of many research projects. In our varying roles as researcher (India Plough) and teacher/assistant to the coordinator of language instruction (Lawrence Kuiper), we recount our experiences in this specific situation, focusing on the various participants and the resulting interpersonal dynamics. By revisiting this project from the multiple perspectives of those involved, we are able to extrapolate several effective strategies for promoting the cooperation that we believe is intrinsic to successful research in a major institution. We hope that this descriptive examination is of use to the seasoned researcher, and we also wish to provide a tool to those who are new to classroom-based research and foresee undertaking a project at a large institution.

THE STUDY

Objective

The research addressed the learnability problem of Second Language Acquisition (SLA), a problem which we are seemingly no closer to solving, given the continued empirical and theoretical debates (Schwartz, 1993; Schwartz & Gubala-Ryzak, 1992; Trahey & White, 1993; White, 1991a, 1991b, 1992a, 1992b) over the roles of positive and negative evidence in SLA. The present study was intended to build on similar work previously done in this area (Trahey & White, 1993; White, 1991a, 1991b, 1992a, 1992b). Specifically, the objective of the research was to investigate the possible role of inductive inferencing in the acquisition of the ungrammaticality of subject–adverb–verb–object word order in French by native speakers of English.

Method

The methodology that was originally developed is as follows. Students learning French as a foreign language, who had not yet been explicitly taught adverb placement in French and who were approximately equivalent in their French proficiency, would be asked to volunteer for the study. All students would be pretested and divided into two groups. For a 2 week period, in Group 1, teaching materials containing adverbs would be integrated into the teacher's regular lesson plans. The intent of these exercises was to provide learners with a "flood" of positive input. In Group 2, in addition to the adverb exercises, the teacher's lessons would be supplemented with verbal inductive inferencing exercises in both French and English. The teacher would be asked not to correct any errors of adverb placement produced by the students, nor was she or he to teach the rule of adverb placement.

All students who volunteered for the study would take three pretests before the 2 week instructional period. Two of these tests, a Word Order Correction (WOC) Task and an Acceptability Judgment (AJ) Task, were adapted from White (1991a, 1992b) and from Trahey and White (1993), and would be used to test students' knowledge of adverb placement in French. The third test was Raven's Standard Progressive Matrices (Raven, 1976), which is a nonverbal test of inductive reasoning.

Immediately following the 2 week instructional period, each group would be posttested using the WOC and AJ Tasks. Three weeks after the first posttest, students would be posttested again to determine any relative long-term effects of the teaching material.

We would like to highlight a number of methodological requirements contained in the original research proposal. Fulfillment of these criteria would minimize the influence of confounding external variables and thus increase the validity of the study. These criteria are as follows: The teacher would not provide explicit instruction with respect to adverb placement in French; the teacher would not correct students' errors of adverb placement in French; students would be exposed to adverbs as much as possible; students would be pretested and posttested; and the researcher would obtain as large a sample size as possible.

The researcher initially requested permission to conduct the study at a local high school. However, she met with resistance, apparently due to a lack of mutual interests, discussed later, and was forced to seek respondents elsewhere. It was decided that the project would be carried out at the researcher's university.

The Institutional Setting. French classes at Michigan State University are taught as part of the Romance and Classical Languages Department, a large department whose curriculum includes French, Spanish, Latin, Classical Greek, Portuguese, and Italian. The department has a lead administrator, the chairperson, who has an assistant chairperson.

This department is in turn under the governance of the College of Arts and Letters, which (as its name suggests) administers the affairs of a great many departments, including that of the researcher, in the University. The College is administered by a Dean and two Associate Deans. The College of Arts and Letters as a unit represents hundreds of faculty members and graduate assistants teaching hundreds of classes per semester to thousands of students.

The College of Arts and Letters is 1 of 14 colleges in the University. In order for any research to be conducted within the University, specific guidelines and procedures must be followed. University policy can be viewed as the overarching or highest tier of hierarchy that the researcher encounters. The University Committee on Research Involving Human Subjects is the review board that must approve all research proposals. Although sometimes considered a mere formality, this application process was unusually difficult in the present case. This issue is discussed later.

The graduate teaching assistants in the French Department are under the supervision of a language coordinator, an individual with a faculty appointment, whose primary roles are to create syllabuses and to schedule teaching duties. With the exception of occasional classroom observations by the coordinator, the teachers remain autonomous with respect to their daily classroom decision making. In addition to the coordinator, there are two assistant coordinator positions held by graduate teaching assistants. In the present case, the assistant coordinator also taught one of the introductory French classes that participated in the study.

Preparatory Stages. Following the advice of a mutual friend, the researcher first approached the assistant coordinator with the proposal in order to discuss the feasibility of conducting the research in the designated French classes and to find out how receptive the teacher and administrators in the department were likely to be to the project. Because the assistant coordinator was a student of Second Language Acquisition, we were able to discuss the entire project — the theoretical underpinnings, the questions addressed, and exactly what would be expected of the teacher. We examined the materials and tests that would be used in the study. Although his response was favorable, it immediately became apparent that it would be necessary to revise both the research design and the anticipated commencement of the study for reasons that are discussed later.

There are four levels of French courses taught at the University. The lower two levels are taught exclusively by teaching assistants. Only professors teach the upper levels. Within each level, anywhere from 1 to 12 sections may be offered, with an enrollment of 10–25 students in each class. Given the knowledge of French (e.g., vocabulary, sentence structure) that would be necessary in order to utilize the materials and tests prepared for the research and the fact that students could not yet know the rule of adverb placement, the choice of level was limited to one. Additionally, there were only four class sections at this level, which limited the sample size available for the study. Furthermore, each section was taught by a different teacher. This introduced a confounding element into the study, a variation in teaching style. Finally, according to the syllabus for the level, adverbs were to be taught the 8th week of the semester, thus adding a time constraint to the research. That is, it was necessary to complete the study before the students were instructed in the grammatical structure.

Although these constraints proved problematic, and in fact affected the previously mentioned criteria, they did not appear to be so severe as to justify terminating the study. Therefore, the researcher and the assistant coordinator together made an appointment to meet with the language coordinator.

When we met with the language coordinator, we explained the entire project from theory to practice. He was extremely enthusiastic about the research but had four valid concerns. First, it would be necessary to receive the department chair's approval, a task which he took on himself. Second, the teachers of the introductory classes would need to be willing to participate in the study. Third, as the students took standardized quizzes and exams, which were given on prearranged days, he wanted to be certain that the lessons would not be altered to such an extent that the teachers could not cover the prescribed material. Additionally, given the constraints of this rigorous schedule, it was not possible to use class time to administer either the pretests or the posttests. Finally, he was concerned with the students' privacy and the teachers' autonomy in the classroom. He therefore could not give blanket approval to observe, videotape, or audio-tape the classes.

Naturally, the last two issues posed several problems for the researcher. First, the researcher would ultimately be responsible for a descriptive summary of the classroom procedures. The research design required that students be neither corrected on adverb placement nor taught the rule of adverb placement. The researcher had to be able to state confidently that these requirements were met. Second, the researcher was concerned that the number of volunteers would be minimal, because students would be asked to take the pretests and posttests outside of class. To solve the problem of volunteer rate, the language coordinator and the teachers worked out several trades to encourage students to volunteer. For each test a student took, he or she could miss one homework assignment without penalty. If a student attended all three tests, he or she could drop his or her lowest quiz score.

Within a day the language coordinator had received the chairperson's approval. At the suggestion of the language coordinator, the researcher and assistant coordinator scheduled a meeting with the teaching assistants. The language coordinator did not want to approach the teachers because he did not want participation in the project to be perceived as a directive from him (see Markee, this volume).

The researcher and the assistant coordinator explained both the theoretical and practical aspects of the research to the other three teachers and showed them specific examples of how their lessons would be altered. Two of the teachers immediately agreed to participate in the study. One teacher initially showed some reluctance. Based on her comments, it became apparent that she misinterpreted the intent of the project. She thought that she was somehow under investigation (see also Rounds, chapter 3). This misinterpretation was understandable given that this teacher was not in the field of Second Language Acquisition nor had she ever been involved in classroom-based research. She seemed to be equating Second Language Acquisition with teaching methodology. If she was doing her job well, then why would one want to investigate her class? The researcher and assistant coordinator again explained to her that the focus of the research was on the students and not on her. This seemed to relieve her anxiety somewhat, and she agreed to participate. However, in the course of the conversation, it was evident that she perceived her students' performance as a direct reflection of her effectiveness as a teacher. Although students could not have asked for a more conscientious teacher, her initial misinterpretation of the research goal and her desire that her students outperform students in the other sections became a concern. There was a danger that the research design might be compromised: This teacher could spend the 2 week instructional period providing the students with explicit rule instruction and overt correction on adverb placement. This interpersonal problem, coupled with the fact that the language coordinator could not approve classroom observations, posed a methodological dilemma. The resolution of this issue is discussed in the next section.

The teachers and the researcher planned a schedule for the pretests, the instructional period, and the two posttests. Recall that the tests could not be administered during the regular class times. This created other complications. Tests had to be offered multiple times on the same day in order to accommodate all of the students. It was not possible for the teachers to attend each of these testing sessions. Therefore, the researcher was responsible for keeping a sign-up sheet at the sessions so that teachers would know which students were taking advantage of the trades that had been arranged. Rooms had to be reserved through the University Scheduling Office, which can be rather difficult once the semester has begun. The information of test times and locations then had to be disseminated to students. The teachers offered to make the announcements and invited the researcher to come to their classes the day before each of the tests to remind the students.

At this point in the organizational stages of the research, the appropriate departmental administrators and teachers had approved the study, the teachers and researcher had selected the classes to be used, and the logistics of test times and locations had been handled. However, the day before the pretest was to be administered, the University Committee on Research Involving Human Subjects (UCRIHS) had not yet approved the project. The researcher consulted with the chair of her dissertation committee, who immediately called the director of UCRIHS. All but one member of the review board had approved the study. The director informed us that he would contact that member. The dissertation chair continued to call the director every 30 minutes and advised the researcher to go to the UCRIHS office. The director finally spoke with the review board member, who apparently had some concerns that the researcher was attempting to hide certain experimental procedures. The director and the researcher discussed the project in detail. Confident that the researcher had indeed disclosed all information on the original application, the director approved the study.

Implementation

Procedure. Each day, beginning several days before the pretest, the teachers described the project to the students in very general terms. Students were told that everything would be revealed to them in detail at the end of the study. Several days before the pretests, the teachers explained to the students that a study was being conducted to investigate how native speakers of English learn French. The teachers outlined the trades that had been worked out and they encouraged students to volunteer. The day before the pretests, the researcher visited each of the classes and repeated the general description of the project to the students. They were asked to be patient and told that if they were informed at this point in time of what was being investigated, the study would be affected. They seemed to accept this. Approximately 65% of the students enrolled in the introductory French classes volunteered to take the pretests.

Teachers were provided with lessons for one week at a time. In their packets were the number of copies of handouts needed for their classes. The goal was to minimize the amount of extra preparation demanded of the teachers and to provide them with relatively long-range instructions. Students (particularly those in Group 2, the inferencing group) were aware that the researcher had prepared some of the lessons, but they did not know how the lessons had been changed. The teachers noted that only a few students asked what the intent of the inductive inferencing exercises was and how other exercises had been changed. The teachers repeated to the students that everything would be explained to them at the end of the study. The teachers and the researcher met daily to discuss how the day's lesson had progressed, which students were absent, and if any revisions in the instructional plan were necessary.

After the first few days of the instructional period, two of the teachers confided that they were having difficulty completing all of the material given to them. Together we revised the lesson plans so that neither research nor instructional goals were compromised. These revised lessons included eliminating some exercises, in addition to allowing the teachers some flexibility in how the exercises were taught. For example, if a lesson originally called for an exercise to be conducted as pair work and the teacher found that class time was running out, the exercise would be taught as a teacher-centered activity, which typically requires less time.

These revisions in the lessons increased the variation in teaching style, which was already a confounding variable in the study as a result of the fact that the sections were taught by four different teachers. This issue could not be ignored. The teachers and the researcher met to attempt to resolve the problem of accounting for differences in material presentation. Ideally, teaching style across classes would be constant. This was impossible in the present case, and it was necessary to describe this variation. All of the teachers understood the dilemma and took the time to fill out relatively elaborate questionnaires regarding each day's class period. Additionally, the one teacher who was somewhat leery of the research in the beginning said the researcher could visit her class at any time.

The remainder of the instructional period progressed without any problems. The day before each of the posttests, at the beginning of class, the teachers announced the test times and locations. The researcher arrived at the end of the class period to remind the students of the test. Of the 45 students who initially volunteered, 42 students followed through to the second posttest, which was 5 weeks after the pretest. After the second posttest, the researcher held special sessions to explain the intent of the research to the students.

DISCUSSION

After reflecting upon the project's administration, which certainly produced complications in the professional lives of all participants, we believe that it can, nevertheless, be characterized as one of cooperation, collaboration, and compromise. These attributes in turn resulted in the successful completion of the project. We suggest that two interdependent ingredients were key to the collaborative nature of the project: The appropriate networks (in terms of "structural and content characteristics," see Milroy, 1987) were utilized, and an open and honest dialogue between all participants was maintained throughout the course of the project. We illustrate that on every level the concept of social network and its inherent principle of exchange may be applied to the implementation of this project.

Understanding and Utilizing Network Concepts

When undertaking a research project, it is necessary to have knowledge and understanding of the networks available in the project's environment. In the present case, the researcher was able to discern one network to which she belonged (graduate students) and one to which she needed access (French department). Mutual recognition of the network is necessary for the network's existence. The first dialogue between the researcher and a representative of the French department took place between the authors of the present chapter. The characteristics of this initial contact proved significant in every phase of the research in three respects. First, the connection between the researcher's network and the teacher's network was created. Second, the particular individuals between which this link was forged is notable. Because we were both graduate students studying Second Language Acquisition at the time, we shared a common role. Importantly, we both tacitly acknowledged our mutual interests, and thus recognized each other's membership in the same network. As a result, an unspoken rapport based on unity, empathy, and reciprocity was immediately established. This mutual recognition immediately became the basis for a system of exchange, even though what was to be gained by such exchange remained undefined. Although nonrecognition of the importance of the research by potential participants led to the peremptory refusal of the project in the high school setting, the commonality of situation and goal between two doctoral candidates at the same institution fostered an alliance. Such artificial boundaries as discipline and department were overridden by the much stronger influence of network membership, which implicitly entailed exchange obligations. If, on the other hand, the researcher had first approached the chairperson of the department, such a shared purpose would have been absent. Additionally, network associations or communications certainly would have developed differently. Whether or not the project would have been hindered or improved as a result remains speculative. Finally, the assistant to the coordinator was the perfect liaison to introduce an outsider into the network of the French department. That is to say, his position within his network was crucial in that he had access to all members of the network and understood the inner workings of the network.

A parallel network system and its corollary system of exchange can be seen in the interactions between the researcher and the teachers. As previously noted, this relationship was mediated by the assistant coordinator who was also a teacher. The assistant coordinator was able to explain to the teachers in insider terms what precisely was expected of them. The researcher could offer concrete exchange items in the form of lesson plans and materials. With these tangible articles, the researcher was able to forego appeals to altruistic, and thus less reliable, predispositions on the part of the teachers and also to establish network ties with the teachers. Importantly, the researcher and the teachers were now communicating directly with each other rather than through the assistant coordinator. This material exchange and direct contact set the groundwork for an eventual relationship of reciprocity characteristic of that shared in the initial contact between the authors. The teachers began to take genuine interest in and ownership of the study.

It was the teachers who gave suggestions for the trades to be offered to the students, thus continuing the series of exchanges upon which the success of the study rested. The students, while receiving grade incentives, brought the system of exchange full circle by providing the researcher with exceptional rates of participation.

Exchange and Interpersonal Dynamics

The four concerns expressed by the coordinator and discussed earlier, reveal some factors which may motivate an administrator to place restrictions on a research project. We recall briefly that the coordinator wanted to make sure that (a) he was being fair to the teachers, (b) that the chair's approval was obtained, (c) that the already planned syllabus was not interfered with, and (d) that the privacy of the students and teachers was not threatened. It may be generalized that the basis for fairness to teachers was the coordinator's relationship to his subordinates. Regard for his superior was reflected in item (b). The coordinator's own professional duties clearly motivate concern (c). Finally, item (d) can be classified as belonging to the personal convictions of the coordinator.

It is evident from the characterization above that to speak in terms of a single agenda on the part of a single player is to simplify the dynamics of professional communication, at least in the university setting. If the above concerns were to be termed the agenda of the coordinator, it is notable that only the fourth item posed a problem to the researcher. The first three served more to aid in the ease of implementation of the project than to hinder it. Items (a) and (c) cleared the path to the teachers by making it manifest in advance that their class routines would not be disrupted. Item (b), which we recall the coordinator took upon himself to handle, was a necessity of which the researcher may not otherwise have been aware.

Although the fourth consideration posed a problem for the validity of the research, it may be argued that, on a principle of exchange, it was generative of what was to become the most positive aspect of the research; the rates of participation and return. The coordinator was aware that by enforcing his own personal convictions, he was in a sense taking away from the researcher. It was at least partially as a result of this that he offered the incentives to students which eventually gave back the exceptional participation and return rates.

Perhaps of most interest to a researcher who needs to approach a person in an administrative position in a large institution is the understanding of the multiple factors that are connected to that person's ability to give what is needed. Knowledge of the dynamics of the hierarchy within which the particular administrator is placed is important. Equally important is evaluating the motivations for concerns and restrictions that this person may make on a project. It is natural to assume that when an exchange occurs between participants in a research project, all of the agents involved in the transaction will expect to benefit in some way. What may be less apparent in the university setting is the considerable exchange value of what can be termed "personal convictions." Part of the mission of a university is the free exchange of ideas. It is important, therefore, to keep in mind not only the principle of exchange upon which network relations are always based, but also the specific network environment that will dictate the type of exchange currency used in the market. Personal convictions are legal tender but their value is nonnegotiable.

Open Dialogue

We wish to make clear that network ties are founded on and maintained through open dialogue. Through direct communication each member makes known her or his opinions, concerns, and agendas, enters into negotiations with other network members, and eventually accomplishes desired goals. Each participant in the present research actively participated in this process of communication, negotiation, and resolution. However, total disclosure of one's motivations, while necessary, is not sufficient for the establishment of these ties. One must bear in mind that as an outsider, one is always suspect. Therefore, one must find a way to assure prospective network members that there are no hidden agendas. Such was the case with one of the teachers who was suspicious of the researcher's investigation. The researcher was able to clarify the intent of the study by freely discussing it with the teacher. Importantly, the progression of this negotiation was facilitated by the fact that the researcher had already gained the trust and approval of other network members. Once the teacher was convinced that all the cards were on the table, the problem was quickly resolved.

Resolving problems where such suspicion is present can be extremely difficult when there are no avenues for exchange. This is exemplified in the petition to UCRIHS. Because the member of the review board who delayed approval and the researcher had no direct contact with each other, open dialogue was impossible. In many cases where there is no open dialogue, misunderstandings follow. In contrast, once the director of UCRIHS and the researcher engaged in

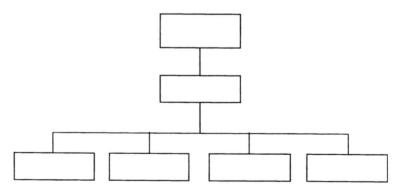

FIG. 5.1. Traditional hierarchy:
The formal bureaucratic model (*de jure*).

face-to-face interaction, the director immediately approved the project. This incident highlights the interrelatedness of network ties and open dialogue. Recall that the researcher initially consulted with her dissertation chair who in turn contacted the director of UCRIHS. This preliminary introduction created a collegial exchange between the director of UCRIHS and the researcher, an exchange which may not have proceeded as efficiently had it been initiated by the researcher alone. This contact was problematic with respect to network relations, but in addition, the university-wide status of UCRIHS as a governing body brings to the fore questions of hierarchy.

Hierarchy Versus Network

Traditional modes of thinking about hierarchy, based on notions of power, do not do justice to present day situations, at least in the case of the university setting. Hierarchical models, such as the one in Fig. 5.1, which depict a pyramid shaped, top to bottom organizational structure, are not applicable to the reality encountered by the participants in the research project described in this chapter. In fact, the most active participants in the success of this project (the students, the teachers, and the researcher) found them-

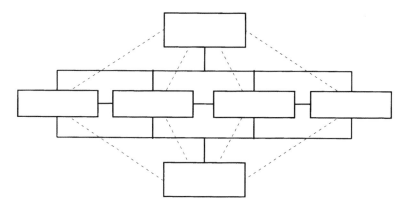

FIG. 5.2. Flattened, nontraditional hierarchy:
The generalized flexible model (*de facto*).

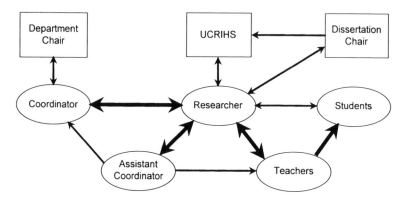

FIG. 5.3. Network dynamics in present study. This representation does not include the negotiated process between the researcher and the dissertation committee preceding and following the actual implementation of the research project.

selves at the bottom of the traditional hierarchical pyramid, with other players distributed in an order that bears no resemblance to the project's actual dynamics. Although the participation of the persons at the top of such a pyramid, the university-level governing body UCRIHS and the chair of the French department, was necessary for the initiation of the project, the roles of these participants remained very much at the periphery of the actual operation of the project. Additionally, no true exchange took place between these officials and other members of the project.

Recently, managerial hierarchies in the private sector have been designed to resemble the image provided by Fig. 5.2. This flattened structure coincides more with the *de facto* conditions in a work environment. The more power-based top to bottom structure has come to be perceived as an artificial imposition that impedes rather than enhances the ability of players to perform (Kohn, 1986). The flattened model, based more on a relationship of reciprocity than on servitude and competition, resembles the kind of network relations that we have tried to exemplify in this chapter.

Figure 5.3 represents a somewhat simplified version of the organizational structure and network dynamics of the present research project. Bold arrows represent a (negotiated) exchange; other arrows represent interaction that involved no immediate effect on the research design.

CONCLUSION

We would like to offer several guidelines which may be useful when conducting classroom-based research at a large institution. We realize that any set of rules, no matter how inclusive, is always an oversimplification of the dynamics of personalities, networks, and hierarchies. We nonetheless believe that certain aspects of our experience may be applicable to situations other than our own.

Researchers, prior to approaching potential participants, will benefit from assessing in detail the networks they need to access. Such an evaluation obviously entails finding an entry point into the network. The choice of network member can be strategically important. It must be a person with whom negotiation is possible. Negotiation and exchange are contingent on mutual goals or interests. Recall the early refusal of the project at the high school. It is probable that this denial was a result of the researcher approaching a network via a member with whom no personal or professional interests were shared. In retrospect, having a better understanding of the high school network and thereby making contact with certain other network members likely would have yielded better results.

It is also to a researcher's advantage to decide in advance which components of the research agenda are negotiable. A continuum could thus be constructed with one extreme representing optimal research conditions and the other end minimal research requirements. In this way the researcher has a clear view of which parts of the project may be compromised in a system of exchange, while bearing in mind those elements that must remain intact.

During the project's implementation, a researcher must therefore be prepared to make use of those items that have been tagged negotiable in order to initiate a series of exchanges that will be advantageous to all participants. Such exchanges are the result as well as the cause of direct and open communication between the researcher and all participants. Such transactions may be termed "compromising" to the research, however, we must remind ourselves that research compromised, but still maintaining predetermined professional standards, is better than no research at all. The present project was successful not only because it met professional standards, but also because of the willingness of all participants to collaborate and to compromise.

ACKNOWLEDGMENTS

We would like to thank the following people for their cooperation and collaboration: Gary Cook, Wayne Cooley, Cheryl Delk, Susan Gass, Stefan Hannuschke, Carolyn Harford, Sabine Helling, Michael Koppisch, Usha Lakshmanan, Mary McCullough, Shawn Morrison, Alya Mousli, Paul Munsell, Jean Nicholas, Keith Palka, Charlene Polio, Dennis Preston, Jacquelyn Schachter, Catherine Tamareille, Amy Tickle, Martha Trahey, Lydia White, David Wright, the Students of French 150, and the College of Arts and Letters for a grant that facilitated the completion of this project.

REFERENCES

Kohn, A. (1986). *No contest: The case against competition.* Boston: Houghton Mifflin.

Milroy, L. (1987). *Language and social networks.* Oxford, England: Blackwell.

Raven, J. (1976). *Raven's Standard Progressive Matrices.* Oxford, England: Oxford Psychologists Press.

Schwartz, B. (1993). On explicit and negative data effecting and affecting competence and linguistic behavior. *Studies in Second Language Acquisition, 15,* 147–163.

Schwartz, B., & Gubala-Ryzak, M. (1992). Learnability and grammar reorganization in L2A: Against negative evidence causing the unlearning of verb movement. *Second Language Research, 8,* 1–38.

Trahey, M., & White, L. (1993). Positive evidence and preemption in the second language classroom. *Studies in Second Language Acquisition, 15,* 181–204.

White, L. (1991a). Adverb placement in SLA: Some effects of positive and negative evidence in the classroom. *Second Language Research, 7,* 133–161.

White, L. (1991b). The verb-movement parameter in second language acquisition. *Language Acquisition, 1,* 337–360.

White, L. (1992a). Long and short verb movement in second language acquisition. *Canadian Journal of Linguistics, 37,* 273–286.

White, L. (1992b). On triggering data in L2 acquisition: A reply to Schwartz and Gubala-Ryzak. *Second Language Research, 8,* 120–137.

Chapter 6

The Balancing Act: Theoretical, Acquisitional, and Pedagogical Issues in Second Language Research

Patricia L. Rounds
Jacquelyn Schachter
University of Oregon

Several experts have claimed that the explicit teaching of grammatical structure plays little or no role in the classroom-based acquisition of a second or foreign language (Felix, 1981; Krashen, 1981, 1982). However, although naturalistic approaches may lead to fluency and communicative ability, others have argued that such approaches cannot carry a learner to the point of grammatical accuracy (Ellis, 1990; Schmidt & Frota, 1986). Others further claim that activities leading to grammatical consciousness on the part of the learner may be the only way to overcome certain types of syntactic deficits in the second language (Fotos, 1993, 1994; Rutherford, 1987; Rutherford & Sharwood Smith, 1988; Sharwood Smith, 1981; White, 1989). One reason for these conflicting opinions is that there is little if any solid evidence to support either side. As Long (1983) pointed out, most studies dealing with this issue have focused on the effects on learning through formal instruction as contrasted with learning through language contact, and it is not known what, if any, role the explicit teaching of grammatical rules played in these studies. A few recent studies have addressed this issue head on (Doughty, 1991; White, 1991; White, Spada, Lightbown, & Ranta, 1991).

We recently went through the process of designing a research project with this problem in mind. We decided to convene a seminar bringing together concepts from psychology, theoretical linguistics, second language acquisition research, and pedagogy in a fruitful manner; our long-term goal for the group was the design of a research project focusing on the issue of grammar teaching within an already established language teaching program. We began with only the certainty that our target population would be adult learners of English in a university-based intensive instructional program. This chapter chronicles the problematic development of that research project, suggesting two ways to approach similarly complex designs: the use of "screens," through which design proposals have to pass, and the development of explicit process strategies for group problem solving.

Descriptions of empirical studies on the issue of the effects of grammar teaching on second language acquisition have generally confined themselves to design questions relating to subjects, teacher training, and length of treatment time. We found that with notable exceptions (Doughty, 1991; Gass, 1982; White et al., 1991), there is little or no discussion of the assumptions made regarding the definition of grammar or how it is that individuals learn. From the outset, we intended to be very specific about these points and to let them lead the development of the study. Thus we found ourselves dedicated to perpetually satisfying several theoretical masters: a linguistic theory of grammar, a psychologically based learning theory, and second language acquisition theory. Further, we insisted that any theoretically oriented design features had to be packaged as pedagogically justifiable classroom materials appropriate to their particular institutional context. Wherever there was not initially a good fit, principled solutions had to be created. Another factor central to our working process was that all seminar participants had to be satisfied that proposals were truly viable and theoretically sound. This was no small feat for two professors, two instructors, and up to six graduate students. In essence, in the way we designed our approach

to this research, we painted ourselves into a very small corner. This chapter describes that corner and suggests a number of strategies we learned for getting out. The nature of
this small corner and the means we realized to find our way
out might be useful to other classroom-based researchers
who are trying to carry out classroom-based principled studies with strong face validity.

THE CONCEPT OF SCREENS

As noted earlier, from the outset of this project we had decided that we wanted to carry out research that was not
only justifiable and interesting from linguistic, psychological, and SLA perspectives, but also pedagogically appropriate. As we read and discussed the pertinent research in
these areas, we found that what might look like a brilliant
proposal from one perspective, would, from another perspective, fail to meet the standards we had set. In the end,
our discard pile was much larger than what found itself
operationalized. This experience led us to conceptualize each
proposal as having to pass through a series of theoretical
and practical screens, each having finer and finer grained
mesh, which essentially ruled out inappropriate proposals.

The Theoretical Screens

The theoretical screens consisted of the three disciplines
we projected would most fruitfully contribute to an answer
to our research problem; linguistics, psychology, and second language acquisition. Any research design would have
to both incorporate an understanding of these areas and
not ignore any major theoretical tenets related to our research question.

Linguistic Theoretical Screen. The notion of grammar has
been largely treated atheoretically in studies designed to
test the effectiveness of teaching it explicitly. This
atheoretical treatment, we argue, contributes to the failure
of other studies to resolve the question of whether explicit
grammar teaching makes any difference. Most studies that

have set out to examine the role of explicit grammar teaching seem to assume an amorphous, undifferentiated body of rules and facts called "grammar" (cf. a review in Ellis, 1990). Grammar is often assumed to be whatever is in the grammar books designed for foreign language students. We realized that one reason why the effect of instruction on grammatical accuracy has not been satisfactorily dealt with may be because not all aspects of what is generally called grammar in foreign language textbooks can or should be approached in the same way. **It may be that instruction in different aspects of grammar need to be approached differently.** For example, teaching the distinction between the present simple and the present progressive in English might involve substantially different approaches and techniques than those involved in helping learners learn to control the structural requirements of wh-questions. The learning burden of the former focuses on the semantics of the different forms, whereas the learning burden of the latter is weighted toward the extraction of the wh-word and the consequent inversion of subject and auxiliary.

To address this deficit, we wanted to begin with an explicit theory of grammar, thus establishing a context that would both help us postulate refined hypotheses about grammar learning and situate our findings. We felt that working within a coherent formalism might lead us to a different set of applied questions; conversely, applied findings might assist in the development of the formalism. Hence, we decided to adopt a Chomskyan view of grammar currently labeled the **Principles and Parameters model** (Chomsky, 1980, 1981, 1991). In this theory, the syntactic component of a grammar is said to have a core and a periphery. **The core consists of two parts;** "principles," which are constraints on the form that grammar can take and which a child comes into the world knowing; and "parameters," which are typological characterizations of possible variation, one variant of which the child fixes via triggering, that is, by the presence of some relevant piece of input. **The grammar also includes a periphery,** which is made up of the exceptional or marked properties of a language; these are properties that must be learned, for example, through generalization. The periphery consists of many aspects of a language which are the result of historical change and bor-rowing, and so forth (cf. White, 1989, for further informa-tion on this model).

Setting out with a particular view of grammar not only grounded us theoretically, but it also began to help us make a choice regarding which grammatical point would become the focus of the study. We knew we wanted to choose a structure that was a reasonable candidate for the core (Baker, 1991; Pollock, 1989). Research on such a structure might enable us to say something about whether the structure was learned or triggered in adult learners. We also wanted to work with a structure that had an established field record, that is, one that theoretical linguists had done a considerable amount of research on, so that we could feel fairly certain that our study would not be made irrelevant by the latest circulating manuscript.

Psychology Theoretical Screen. We felt that most extant studies on the role of explicit grammar teaching suffered from the lack of a well-articulated theory of the process of learning. To address this deficit, we turned to the current work on sequence and artificial language learning by cogni-tive psychologists. The most relevant body of work seemed to be that investigating the roles of attention and aware-ness in sequence learning.[1] On awareness, we relied on the work of Allport (1988) and Tomlin and Villa (1994), in which awareness was operationally assessed by noting both a be-havioral change and the subject's ability to report some ex-perience related to it. For the notion of attention, we adopted the characterization by Posner and Petersen, described in Tomlin and Villa (1994), as having three components; alert-ness, orientation, and focus. We agreed with Tomlin and Villa's claim that none of the components of attention re-quires awareness and we viewed them as separate concepts.

For learning, we relied on the work of several cognitive

---

[1]We realize our focus on attention and awareness does not directly address the question of a learning process. We claim, however, that is-sues involving attention and awareness are integral to any characteriza-tion of that process.

researchers (Cohen, Ivry, & Keele 1990; Curran & Keele, 1993; Nissen & Bullemer, 1987; Schacter 1987) which distinguished between attentional and nonattentional learning, under conditions in which sequences were hierarchically coded in specific ways. In sum, we were able to devise three learning conditions for our study; (+) awareness and (+) attention, (-) awareness and (+) attention, and (-) attention. (-) awareness

SLA Theoretical Screen. In the SLA literature, Krashen (1976, 1981, 1982) established the major theoretical camp regarding explicit grammar teaching by making a distinction between learning a language and learning about a language, a distinction he characterized as acquisition and learning. He claimed that only acquisition, which is an unconscious process that occurs when an individual tries to understand input containing a structure, contributes to second language development. Attention to the meaning of the utterance in which the structure occurs is required, in Krashen's view; attention to the structure to be acquired is neither required nor helpful. Learning, which is the development of conscious explicit knowledge of grammar, is only useful for monitoring and editing. More recently, Krashen and Terrell (1983) claimed that the explicit provision of rules can also act as an advance organizer, helping learners notice features of the input; it can also help learners notice the gap between the input they receive and their own output. In the noninterface version of the monitor model (Ellis 1993; Krashen, 1982, and elsewhere), what is explicitly learned cannot become implicit; in weaker versions of the theory, explicit learning can become implicit (Ellis, 1993). White et at. (1991) countered this argument, claiming that learning via a focus on form (not necessarily rules) can lead to the development of syntax and, in fact, may be necessary to avoid early fossilization.

Of course, we decided that we wanted to enter this debate. In other words, we wanted to have data that would tell us whether an explicitly learned structure could become part of implicit knowledge; we also wanted to know whether students could evidence an improved knowledge of structures which were presented only in the context of comprehensible input à la Krashen. Given these arguments and the distinctions in learning presented earlier, we felt we were ready to make a contribution to the discussion.

Practical Screen

Pedagogical Screen. However, it would not be sufficient for our study to be simply sound theoretically. We wanted it to be pedagogically appropriate. Because this research was essentially an examination of how best to affect change in learners, it was in large part a study of the efficacy of a range of teaching techniques. For our results to be most relevant to teachers, the treatments that we utilized in our experiment needed to replicate techniques that teachers might use in the classroom. Even though the research has not provided an answer to the issue of whether explicit grammar teaching makes a difference, language teachers have had to make a choice in the design of their programs. Language programs have traditionally adopted two basic solutions to address the teaching of grammar: There are those who follow an orthodox communicative approach and eschew explicit grammar classes, relying instead on the provision of copious comprehensible input, and there are those who offer a modified version of the communicative approach, retaining a grammar class or devoting a certain amount of class time to explicit, form-focused grammatical explanations and exercises. These more traditional approaches can be further grossly categorized as either deductive, in which a rule is presented, then practiced, as in various cognitive code approaches, or as inductive, such as the audiolingual method in which learners are flooded with a certain kind of data and then led to formulate their own rules, which are said to be attained by the manipulation of sentences containing the target structure (cf. Celce-Murcia, 1991). Others (White et al., 1991) have argued that consciousness raising activities which draw the learner's attention to properties of the L2 by focusing on form can bring about genuine changes in learner performance. In our best case scenario, our project design would include these three general extant treatments.

Another issue related to pedagogy was the question of

whether what teachers were supposed to be doing, for example, teaching communicatively or deductively, was actually what they did, and only what they did. For example, in a comparison of three classes from the same adult communicative ESL program, Spada (1987) found that from time to time teachers would include explicit explanation or provision of rules; one class spent as much as 38% of its time on activities with a primary focus on code. We reasoned that uncontrolled methods of input would lead to questionable findings. Thus, it became paramount for us to figure out some way of controlling input presentation. Eventually we decided to present the grammar lessons within the context of computerized reading/writing lessons.

Institutional Screen.   A third category of screen through which any design proposal must pass is what we call an institutional screen. This screen includes factors related to teachers and students and to the organization they work in.

For face validity, a study on the efficacy of classroom procedures ought to take place in a classroom. However, classrooms are ongoing communities in which teachers and students do their work; often, the researcher is a tolerated guest (Rounds, 1993, this volume). Even in an institute where the researchers teach, they are guests in another teacher's classroom. That classroom ecology is not theirs; the teachers and students in the various classrooms have established their mutual duties and responsibilities independently. Any changes we might request in the pursuit of furthering knowledge would inevitably disrupt those classrooms. Our goal, then, was to figure out a way to minimize disruptions as much as possible.

Further, we have all experienced some classes in which we "clicked" with the students, and others in which it seemed that no matter what we did, the classes seemed to drag. This aspect of affect is delicate and can be damaged by a perceived negative word or glance. Add another individual to the relationship—a third wheel—and you have a good possibility of things going badly. Minimizing our physical and spiritual presence was added to our list of concerns.

There were also questions about the face validity of the

study from the student point of view. Students come to our institutes and classrooms with certain expectations and ideas about how the business of language learning and teaching ought to go. Teachers routinely engage in learner training, as, for example, in training students who are accustomed to teacher-fronted, sentence-based instruction, to accept and thrive in more student-oriented, communicative classrooms. However, such training generally occurs over an extended period of time in a secure environment in which teachers and students regularly and consistently engage in the teaching/learning process. We, on the other hand, would probably not be making an extended commitment to the education of the students involved in our project; thus, we needed to make sure that whatever we asked them to do would be seen by them as being valuable in their job of learning a second language. Unusual demands or techniques, however theoretically justified, would have to be weighed against this human factor. Overall continuity in the program had to be preserved whenever possible. Besides, students were paying money for these courses; we had to deliver an appropriate program.

We were also faced with a number of concerns both internal and external to our institute. Consideration of the issues of time and money to be devoted to the project was unavoidable; as much as research ought to remain "pure," the amount of time and money individuals and institutions have to devote to it is rather small. Teachers and students have heavy demands placed on their time, so we felt constrained to limit our requests of them. The researchers, who were also teachers and graduate students, felt similar demands. We could further anticipate that money to buy equipment, and time for materials development would be limited. Even the issue of scheduling came into play. Teachers who wanted to be part of the research effort would have to be scheduled to teach the targeted class; the researchers had to be scheduled to be able to work with or observe the teachers. Any changes in the usual schedule of classes had to be dealt with.

Some of the concerns we had to anticipate related to our institute's position as a university entity. Any special classroom needs had to be scheduled well in advance and through the established channels (see also Kuiper & Plough, chapter 5). Scheduling needs were monitored both logistically (Did the university have the rooms?) and in terms of impact (Would scheduling one set of classes bar other programs from using certain facilities?). Another constraint related to our campus status was the requirement that we pass a human subjects review. Although we did not anticipate any problems with such a review, it was a factor we had to consider both in terms of design of the project and in terms of getting the review through channels expeditiously (see Kuiper & Plough, chapter 5).

By now the reader may wonder how anyone could do any research at all with so many issues to be considered. It is clear to us that in addition to the pressure to get the theoretical business worked out correctly, classroom-based research entails a very large number of human and institutional factors that can affect research design and outcomes in many unforeseen and unforeseeable ways. It is not for the timid.

Issues, Screens, and Group Processes

As we worked to design a theoretically principled experiment, we faced a number of issues related to the screens we established that in the end entailed various methods of resolution. We believe the discussion of some of these issues will exemplify a set of problem-solving strategies that can be useful to other researchers.

Strategy A: Process of Elimination. The first issue we had to deal with was choosing the grammatical item to teach. This item had to pass through all our screens. From a pedagogical perspective, it had to be something that was not usually part of a structural syllabus so that we could ensure as much as possible that our subjects had not already learned a rule for it; yet it had to be something worth teaching so that we could justify taking time out from their regular classes. From a linguistic screen perspective, the structure had to be part of what would be viewed within the Principles and Parameters framework as part of the core, and not something the linguistic theoreticians would dismiss as being part of the periphery. From a cognitive science perspective, because the parallel we were working on related to artificial language and sequence learning (Carr & Curran, 1994), the grammatical item had to be strictly syntactic, that is the formation of the structure had to be essentially formally expressible and the function had to be something the subjects already knew. Some initial candidates that met the cognitive science screen were: reflexives, conditionals, ordering of adjectives, indirect speech, relative clauses, cleft sentences, comparatives and superlatives of adjectives, and wh-extraction in question formation. However, except for wh-extraction, all of these structures failed to pass through the pedagogical screen because they were central to standard grammar curricula. Wh-extraction seemed to be an excellent candidate linguistically because quite a bit of research already exists on it, and we are reasonably sure that it is governed by a principle and part of the core. In the end we decided to focus on wh-question formation from two- and three-clause sentences, extracting subjects and objects.

Strategy B: Reconceptualization. Another early issue in the design of the project was the nature of the experimental conditions. As previously explained, we decided to focus on the notions of attention and awareness, and hence wanted to have conditions that would reflect these binary oppositions; Condition 1– (+) attention, (+) awareness; Condition 2– (+) attention, (-) awareness; and Condition 3– (-) attention, (-) awareness.

We decided that attention was to be operationalized by having the students manipulate sentences containing the target structure; awareness was to be operationalized by presenting the subjects with a rule and requiring that they manipulate sentences according to the rule. Condition 1 was easy to design, as it represented the kind of deductive grammar exercise students could find in any traditional grammar textbook; a rule is explained, and then students are given a number of examples for practice in manipulating according to the rule. Condition 1 easily passed through both the cognitive psychology and the pedagogical screens. Condition 2 also represented a fairly traditional condition for exposure. Flooding students with a particular type of data and anticipating that they will formulate their own rule is typical of inductive approaches. It meets the (+) attention criterion because students are manipulating the particular structures, and it meets the (-) awareness condition as they are not told there is any rule, nor are they explicitly asked to formulate one.

Design of Condition 3 was much trickier. We wanted students to have the same amount of exposure to the target sentences in all three conditions, so the students in Condition 3 had to have the same amount of visual and aural access to the targets. However, we could not ask them to perform any grammatical manipulations of the sentences as this would constitute at the least an attentional condition. We decided to have them find a synonym in the text for an underlined word in the target sentence. We felt that this would satisfy our attention and awareness criteria. At the same time, it passed through the pedagogical screen as it would essentially be a comprehensible input condition because the students would need to focus on the meaning of the total sentence in order to choose the appropriate synonym. We were pleased. However, when we presented our design to a cognitive science research group, they were unhappy on two accounts. First, they felt that simply reading and hearing the sentences was insufficient; they wanted the students to process the material behaviorally. This objection was readily answered by asking the students to read their answers out loud. Their second objection was more problematic. They felt we needed what is called a "distractor" task, that is one in which subjects are performing two tasks at the same time, so that they were prevented from paying attention to the target sentences, or at least their attention to the sequential syntax is degraded. Eventually we devised the following condition: Students would see a word on the computer screen for a certain amount of time; they would be asked to memorize the word; then, the word would disappear from the screen and a sentence would appear. The students had to begin reading the sentence out loud as soon as it appeared, replacing the appropriate word in the sentence with the word they had memorized. The two-task condition thus consisted of remembering the word, while trying to figure out where to place it in the sentence. The psychologists were happy with this condition. However, it did not seem to pass through the pedagogical screen. We wanted our results to be interesting to second language teachers as well as to cognitive scientists. We wanted to know if the students could improve their knowledge of a structure without paying attention to it, but the situation would have to have some face validity for teachers. At first, we could not imagine that a teacher would ask students to perform such a task in a real classroom. We were at a crossroads. Then it occurred to us that this task was similar to a slot-filler exercise, that is an exercise in which the student had to remember a sentence and then substitute in that sentence a word cue provided by the teacher. This was a variation on that theme: The student would have to remember a word cue, not a sentence. Furthermore, students would be focused on the meaning of the sentence when they were asked to do the substitution, so in essence this condition could be considered a variant of the comprehensible input condition. Last, they would read the new sentence out loud, satisfying the earlier behavioral objection and providing consistency on this point through all conditions. From this dual reconceptualization, our Condition 3 was able to pass through both the pedagogical and cognitive science screens.

Strategy C: Buckshot. Not all issues could be so elegantly solved. Sometimes a problem had to have multiple solutions. The question of what would count as having learned the target structure was one such question. From the linguistic point of view, a change in linguistic competence is appropriate, and is most commonly gauged via grammaticality judgments. However, from the pedagogical point of view, a change in linguistic performance in spoken and written behavior is desired, and should be judged via some performance eliciting device. And from the point of view of the psychologist, subjective behavior (i.e., grammaticality judgments) was insufficient; it had to be supplemented by objective behavior, thus necessitating the use of reaction time data. But we also felt constrained to limit the number of tests and testing devices used in order not to stress our subjects unduly.

Argument between the (linguistic) grammaticality judgment advocates in our group and the (pedagogical) performance advocates especially seemed to yield no middle ground. In the end we employed a battery of tests, compromising most significantly on the effect such a battery might have on subjects' affect. Because some of the tests were administered outside of class time, we tried to lessen the multiple test effect by offering a prize to all who completed the tests, a nicely designed university T-shirt—a hot item, as it turned out.

We gave three types of tests, each of which took about 20–25 minutes to administer. To pass through our linguistic screen we gave a grammaticality judgment test tied to reaction time data, making it also pertinent to the psychology screen. This test was administered four times during the 4-week training period: at the start of training, halfway through training, at the end of training, and a week after training ended. For our pedagogical screen, we adopted a production task from the psychological framework, namely elicited imitation via delayed recall. Such a test is designed to measure the implicit knowledge that accounts for accuracy and automaticity in comprehension and production, rather than the explicit knowledge that might come into play in more traditional pen and pencil tasks. We felt that this implicit knowledge was what teachers were ultimately seeking to help students attain, and that its demonstration in a production task would pass the pedagogical screen. In an elicited imitation task, a subject is presented with a string of words and asked to repeat it in order to allow the researcher to make inferences about the subject's knowledge of the language. If the sentence exceeds the capacity of the working memory (7 ± 2 units), then it can only be repeated if grammar is available to organize the information into chunks. Although many researchers such as Chaudron and Bley-Vroman (1994) argue that elicited imitation is a valid tool for measuring an individual's general ability to control a grammar, recent research by Yang (1993) suggests that delayed recall is a more sensitive and accurate tool for evaluating a second language learner's control of grammar because performance of delayed repetition is clearly not a simple artifact of working memory. Subjects must store the proposition in long-term memory while they perform a distractor task, then reconstruct the sentence using their own internal grammar after the distractor task has been completed. Hence, we felt that delayed repetition offered a means of gauging students' competence via a performance task, thus satisfying both linguists and teachers.

Finally, we administered a production task that we felt would appear to be valid to the students, because it was designed to approximate one use of the target structure in communicative situations. The students were oriented in the following way: "When you are talking with an American, sometimes you can only hear part of a sentence. If you don't quite understand a word or an important piece of information, it is useful to ask a clarifying question. For example, if you hear me say, 'John won XXXX (garbled word)!' you might ask 'What did John win?' to find out the missing piece of information." Students were given several sentences with garbled words and asked to provide the appropriate clarifying questions. Again, this was an oral test, because we still wanted to avoid providing unlimited time for students to access explicit rules they might have. This test was also administered immediately before training began and after it ended.

We felt it would have been more elegant and less taxing to test student performance with one, well-designed test. However, the goal of elegance had to be subsumed by a more piecemeal solution, which we felt would more accurately and appropriately capture change.

Strategy D: Fiat.   Not all design issues could be solved democratically. Sometimes a conflict needed to be solved by fiat. The question of feedback was such an issue. It was extremely clear to the more practice oriented of the researchers that feedback was an essential feature of any second language class and that students expected feedback; this group felt that for the project design to have any validity for teachers, feedback needed to be provided. It was equally as clear to the more theory oriented of the researchers that providing feedback would not pass through the second language acquisition screen, as getting an answer to the question of whether pattern learning could occur under these three conditions would be confounded by the introduction of feedback. It was further argued that feedback has not been found to be systematically provided in communicative classrooms, and, hence, was not really as central to classroom behavior as imagined by the opposing group (cf. Schachter, 1991). This set of arguments did not appease the practice-oriented group; the language acquisition-oriented group felt equally certain that providing any feedback would taint the data. The group was at an impasse. In the end, somebody had to become the boss. She declared that there would be no feedback in this experiment. The importance of this issue was noted, though, and an agreement was arrived at—that the very next experiment would address that issue.

CONCLUSION

We found the conceptualization of screens and the development of strategy types outlined here to be useful to us in the formulation of our research project. Having an explicit notion of these process matters provided us with a set of tools for working through the various design stages of our project. As we have noted, at times the sheer number of factors that had to be weighed and considered was daunting. During this, our first attempt at working with a large and diverse group of collaborators, we could always depend on someone to remember this or the other factor. There were times when we thought we had perfected a design feature only to have it scuttled by one of our temporarily forgotten factors, sending us back to rethink and replan. However, even when we were in the thick of the design discussion, we were always amazed that no matter how hopeless a situation would seem, eventually a solution would suggest itself. Armed now with a metaunderstanding of how solutions can be found we hope to be more efficient at finding them. As to the experiment itself, we leave judgment on that to the reader.

REFERENCES

Allport, A. (1988). What concept of consciousness? In A. J. Marcel & E. Bisiach (Eds.), *Consciousness in contemporary science* (pp. 159–182). London: Clarendon Press.

Baker, L. (1991). The syntax of English *not*: The limits of core grammar. *Linguistic Inquiry, 22,* 387–429.

Carr, T. H., & Curran, T. (1994). Cognitive factors in learning about structured sequence: Applications to syntax [special issue]. *Studies in Second Language Acquisition, 16,* 205–230.

Celce-Murcia, M. (1991). Grammar pedagogy in second and foreign language teaching. *TESOL Quarterly, 25,* 459–480.

Chaudron, C., & Bley-Vroman, R. (1994). Elicited imitation as a measure of second-language competence. In E. E. Tarone, S. M. Gass, & A. D. Cohen (Eds.), *Research methodology in second-language acquisition* (pp. 245–261). Hillsdale, NJ: Lawrence Erlbaum Associates.

Chomsky, N. (1980). *Rules and representations.* Oxford, England: Basil Blackwell.

Chomsky, N. (1981). *Lectures on government and binding.* Dordrecht: Foris.

Chomsky, N. (1991). Some notes on economy of derivation and representation. In R. Freiden (Ed.), *Principles and parameters in comparative grammar* (pp. 417–454). Cambridge, MA: MIT Press.

Cohen, A., Ivry, R. I., & Keele, S. W. (1990). Attention and structure in sequence learning. *Journal of Experimental Psychology: Learning, Memory, and Cognition 16,* 17–30.

Curran, T., & Keele, S. W. (1993). Attentional and nonattentional forms of sequence learning. *Journal of Experimental Psychology: Learning, Memory, and Cognition, 19,* 189–202.

Doughty, C. (1991). Second language instruction does make a difference. *Studies in Second Language Acquisition, 13,* 431–469.

Ellis, R. (1990). *Instructed second language learning.* Oxford, England: Basil Blackwell.

Ellis, R. (1993). The structural syllabus and second language acquisition. *TESOL Quarterly, 27,* 91–113.

Felix, S. W. (1981). The effect of formal instruction on second language acquisition. *Language Learning, 31,* 87–112.

Fotos, S. (1993). Consciousness raising and noticing through focus on form: Grammar task performance versus formal instruction. *Applied Linguistics, 14,* 385–407.

Fotos, S. (1994). Integrating grammar instruction and communicative language use through grammar consciousness-raising tasks. *TESOL Quarterly, 28,* 323–351.

Gass, S. (1982). From theory to practice. In M. Hines & W. Rutherford (Eds.), *On TESOL '81* (pp. 129–139). Washington, DC: Teachers of English to speakers of Other Languages.

Krashen, S. D. (1975). The essential contributions of formal instruction in adult second language learning. *TESOL Quarterly, 9,* 173–183.

Krashen, S. D. (1976). Formal and informal linguistic environments in language acquisition and language learning. *TESOL Quarterly, 10*, 157–168.

Krashen, S. D. (1981). *Second language acquisition and second language learning.* Oxford, England: Pergamon.

Krashen, S. D. (1982). *Principles and practice in second language acquisition.* Englewood Cliffs, NJ: Prentice-Hall.

Krashen, S. D., & Terrell, T. D. (1983). *The natural approach.* Englewood Cliffs, NJ: Alemany Press.

Long, M. H. (1983). Does second language instruction make a difference? A review of research. *TESOL Quarterly, 17*, 359–382.

Nissen, M. J., & Bullemer, P. (1987). Attentional requirements of learning: Evidence from performance measures. *Cognitive Psychology, 19*, 1–32.

Pollock, J-Y. (1989). Verb movement, universal grammar, and the structure of IP. *Linguistic Inquiry, 20*, 365–424.

Rounds, P. L. (1993, August). *Applied linguistics fieldwork: a case of a stranger in a strange land.* Paper presented at AILA Conference, Amsterdam.

Rutherford, W. (1987). *Second language grammar: Learning and teaching.* London: Longman.

Rutherford, W., & Sharwood-Smith, M. (Eds.). (1988). *Grammar and second language teaching.* New York: Newbury House.

Schachter, J. (1991). Corrective feedback in historical perspective. *Second Language Research, 7*, 89–102.

Schacter, D. (1987). Implicit memory: History and current status. *Journal of Experimental Psychology, 13*, 501–518.

Schmidt, R., & Frota, S. N. (1986). Developing basic conversational ability in a second language: A case study of an adult learner of Portuguese. In R. Day (Ed.), *Talking to learn: conversation in second language acquisition* (pp. 237–326). Rowley, MA: Newbury House.

Sharwood Smith, M. (1981). Consciousness raising and the second language learner. *Applied Linguistics, 2*, 159–168.

Spada, N. (1987). Relationships between instructional differences and learning outcomes: A process-product study of communicative language teaching. *Applied Linguistics, 8*, 137–161.

Tomlin, R., & Villa, V. (1994). Attention in cognitive science and SLA [special issue]. *Studies in Second Language Acquisition, 16*, 183–203.

White, L. (1989). *Universal grammar and second language acquisition.* Amsterdam: John Benjamins.

White, L. (1991). Adverb placement in second language acquisition: Some effects of positive and negative evidence in the classroom. *Second Language Research, 7*, 133–161.

White, L., Spada, N., Lightbown, P., & Ranta, L. (1991). Input enhancement and L2 Question formation. *Applied Linguistics, 12*, 416–432.

Yang, L. R. (1993). *The acquisition of a second language under controlled experimental conditions.* Unpublished doctoral dissertation, University of Oregon.

Chapter 7

Making Second Language Classroom Research Work

Numa Markee
University of Illinois at Urbana-Champaign

The chapters in this book all have as their topic second language classroom research (SLCR). Contrary to what might be called mainstream SLCR, however, they do not report on the results of experiments of either developmental or analytical studies. Rather, they focus on what Duff and Early (chapter 1) call the "problematics" of conducting SLCR. What makes these chapters particularly interesting is that problematics are so rarely discussed in the mainstream SLCR literature. The problematics of conducting SLCR identified in this book include a wide range of factors, such as the impact of various sociocultural constraints on the research enterprise; the role of SLCR as a tool for implementing social change (whether in a society as a whole or in the more restricted context of a single classroom); the importance of good communication between the various stakeholders who participate in educational change; the importance of resolving questions such as who "owns" project data and any resulting classroom applications; and, last but not least, the costs and benefits that may accrue to different project participants from adopting or rejecting educational innovations.

It is important to note that the writers of these chapters do not disdain the noteworthy achievements of mainstream research in SLCR, to which, as Duff and Early note, they have themselves contributed. However, there is a clear distinction between the kind of research on which all these writers report in this collection and mainstream SLCR. A great deal of mainstream SLCR has concentrated on explaining the interrelationships between process and product in instructed second language acquisition (SLA). Moreover, this process–product research has been predominantly quantitative in orientation and has typically focused rather narrowly on linguistic and other issues in instructed SLA, such as the types of questions teachers ask of learners (Banbrook & Skehan, 1990; Brock, 1986; Long & Sato, 1983; White & Lightbown, 1984) or the effect of task type on learner production (Doughty & Pica, 1986; Duff, 1986, 1993; Long, 1989a; Long & Porter, 1985; Pica, Holiday, Lewis, & Morgenthaler, 1989; Pica, Young, & Doughty, 1987; Porter, 1986). Thus, mainstream SLCR has not addressed the kinds of "sociology of SLCR" issues identified in the previous paragraph.

By addressing these broader sociological issues, the authors of these chapters break new ground in SLCR in at least two ways. First, we note the emerging epistemological shift (most noticeable in the Duff and Early chapter) toward a greater appreciation of the contribution that qualitatively oriented action research can make to SLCR. And second, we note the interest expressed so clearly in nearly all chapters in adopting a more engaged approach to making social change actually happen.

It is striking how similar these researchers' concerns and discourse are to those of writers who have analyzed the problems of implementing curricular change from the theoretical perspective of how and why innovations diffuse, a perspective which, though still largely unfamiliar to applied linguists, is beginning to make increasingly frequent appearances in the SL curriculum development literature (see Bailey, 1992; Beretta, 1990; Brindley & Hood, 1991; Candlin, 1984a, 1984b; Henrichsen, 1989; Holliday, 1992, 1994; Holliday & Cooke, 1982; Hutchin, 1992; Kennedy, 1987, 1988; Markee, 1986a, 1986b, 1993, 1994b, 1994c; Stoller, 1992, 1994; White, 1988; White, Martin, Stimson, & Hodge,

1991 and Young, 1993). Thus, the focus of this chapter is to show the profitable links that can be made between the kind of SLCR outlined in the Duff and Early; Spada, Ranta, and Lightbown; and Rounds chapters in this volume and a diffusion of innovations perspective on managing educational change.

More specifically, in Part 1 of this chapter, I outline how the kinds of issues raised by these chapters may be integrated into a diffusionist framework, one that allows us to understand the different ways in which knowledge may be constructed and utilized. This discussion serves to locate qualitative action research on a continuum of models and strategies for implementing social change and to highlight the advantages and disadvantages of action research vis-a-vis other approaches to making change happen. In Part 2, in the spirit of this volume's call for more explicit discussions of the problematics of SLCR, I then discuss the practical problems encountered in the process of trying to institutionalize action research by ESL teaching assistants (TAs) at a research university in the United States.[1] In addition, I outline the solutions that were devised and discuss the relative successes and failures of these solutions. The activities reported on in this chapter are part of a larger project in curricular and teacher innovation that I refer to as the CATI project.

This project aims to promote curriculum development in a university-level ESL program by developing the professional skills of the TAs who teach the program's courses. This objective entails engaging TAs who are concurrently working toward a MATESL degree in a broad range of syllabus design and materials development activities and research. The TAs' syllabus design and materials development activities have already been described in Markee (1994b) and are not described in any great detail here. Instead, I concentrate on showing how action research by TAs can potentially empower these teachers to construct their own theories of SL teaching, theories that are both theoretically informed and relevant to their own experiences of teaching

---

[1]ESL Teaching Assistants are full-time graduate students who are employed on a part-time basis to teach ESL classes to international students.

and learning at this institution. But as we will see, achieving such an objective is surprisingly complex.

PART 1. CURRICULAR INNOVATION: DEFINITIONS AND EXAMPLES

Elsewhere (see Markee, 1993; in press), I have outlined in some detail a framework for analyzing curricular innovation in second language teaching (see Cooper, 1982; 1989, for the framework's intellectual origins). This framework analyzes social change in terms of the following multidimensional question: "Who adopts what, where, when, why, and how?" The constituent elements of this question allow us to understand:

- The wide range of individuals who potentially have a stake in any change, and the socially defined roles they play in the adoption process (who).
- The stages and kinds of decision-making processes that potential adopters typically go through as they evaluate whether to adopt or reject an innovation (adopts).
- The characteristics of innovations (what).
- The influence of sociocultural context on diffusion–specifically, the roles played by cultural, political, institutional, and various other systemic constraints in determining the success or failure of classroom innovations (where).
- The time-bound nature of the diffusion process, which may be described in terms of three distinct phases which are characterized by different rates of adoption[2] (when).

---

[2]In the case of successful innovations, the process of adoption characteristically begins quite slowly as a small minority of the members of a social system (for example, a department, a school, or a national education system) start to adopt an innovation. The rate of adoption then picks up speed as a "jumping onto the bandwagon" effect comes into play and the majority of individuals in the system adopt the innovation. And finally, the rate of adoption tapers off as fewer and fewer potential adopters in the system remain to adopt the innovation.

- The impact of personality variables associated with different kinds of adopters (early, majority, and late) and the importance of the perceived attributes of an innovation (such as its relative advantage to potential adopters); according to circumstance, these factors either inhibit or encourage end users to adopt a proposed change (why).
- The structural mechanisms involved in the diffusion of innovations and the different models and strategies of change that may be used to manage the implementation of curricular innovation (how).

In the rest of part 1, I focus on the theoretical issues that pertain to the what, why, and how parts of this framework. In Part 2, where I discuss the CATI project, I refer to issues that are covered by the other constituent elements of the framework outlined above.

What, Why, and How

Curricular innovation is a process of development that focuses on managing the design, implementation, and maintenance of educational change. Its key dimensions are the development of teaching (and/or testing) materials, methodological skills, and pedagogical values, which are perceived as new by individuals who make up a formal (language) education system. For reasons of focus, I do not propose to discuss all the implications of this definition here; however, let me briefly elaborate on three aspects of this definition that allow us to consider the what, the why, and the how of curricular innovation in an integrated fashion.

First, the core of all curricular innovation in language education is the development by teachers of new materials, methodological skills, and pedagogical values (Fullan, 1982a; 1982b; 1993). Of these three core dimensions of change, the development by teachers of new methodological skills and pedagogical values constitutes potentially fruitful areas for action research by teachers themselves. Second, "newness" is a relative, not an absolute concept

(Markee, 1993; Nicholls, 1983; Rogers, 1983).[3] And third, curricular innovation as defined above goes hand in hand with organization development (Everard & Morris, 1990; Schmuck, 1982). That is, teachers' innovative activities in the areas of developing new materials, methodological skills, and pedagogical values must be adequately supported by the organization to which they belong. This systemic linkage frequently requires the organization to develop its own capacity in order to sustain an on-going CATI project. I develop these three points further in Part 2.

Models and Strategies of Change

What is action research? How does it differ from other forms of research? And how does it promote the implementation of curricular innovation? Innovation and action research are in fact closely related concepts: Action research is essentially a particular way of promoting educational change (Chin & Benne, 1976; Havelock, 1971; Markee, 1993; White, 1988). More specifically, as shown in Table 7.1, we may distinguish among three models of change. As we will see, the social interaction model depicts unplanned change whereas both the research, development, and diffusion (RD&D) and problem-solving models are associated with specific strategies for implementing planned change. For the sake of expository simplicity, I refer to such models and strategies as approaches to change.

The Social Interaction Model. The social interaction model is a model of how spontaneous change occurs. There is therefore no explicit strategy for making planned change happen

---

[3]Thus, although action research has a long history in education (going back to Dewey, 1904) and is therefore not new in any objective sense, it is a rather recent development in second and foreign language teaching (Crookes, 1993). To the extent that action research is subjectively perceived as new by individual language teachers who do not yet know much about it, it counts for them as a bona fide innovation in its own right. Similarly, the introduction of a course in action research will count as an innovation in graduate programs which do not currently offer such a course, particularly if it is proposed that this course is to have required rather than elective status.

TABLE 7.1
Models and associated strategies of change

Models of change	Strategies of change
Social interaction	N/A
RD&D	Empirical–rational and/or Power–coercive
Problem solving	Action Research

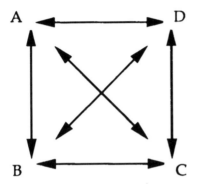

FIG. 7.1. A communication network.

in association with it. This model emphasizes the importance of social relationships as a key variable in adoption.
The major insight offered by this model to students of innovation in educational contexts (where change is hopefully
planned) is that it emphasizes the crucial role played by
both communication and communication networks in promoting or inhibiting the diffusion of innovations (Cooper
1982; 1989). As shown in Fig. 7.1, a communication network consists of a group of individuals, in which A, B, C,
and D know and habitually communicate with each other
either face-to-face or by telephone, electronic mail, or traditional means of written communication.

Communication networks are essential if innovations are
to diffuse. As shown in Fig. 7.2, an innovation is able to
spread from Network 1 to Network 2 because D and E know
each other. Once E knows what D knows about innovation
X, she or he can then share this information with F, G, and
H in Network 2. Thus, the process of diffusion is funda-

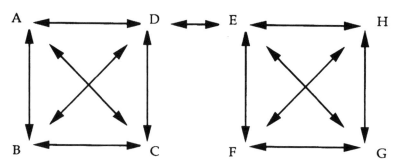

FIG. 7.2. The spread of innovation between two
communication networks (Cooper, 1989).

mentally a process of communication (Rogers, 1983).

In contrast, the two remaining approaches to change shown in Table 7.1 are concerned with implementing planned change. As such, they have identifiable strategies for making change happen which are clearly associated with them. Thus, the RD&D model is associated with empirical–rational and power–coercive strategies of innovation while the problem-solving model employs an action research strategy to achieve change.

The RD&D Model Empirical–Rational Strategy. The RD&D model, which is predominant in academia and in a variety of industries ranging from the space/defense industry to agribusiness, is rational, systematic, and theory-based. It tends to be used in conjunction with an empirical–rational strategy but is sometimes also associated with a power–coercive strategy of change. In its classic form, the former strategy assumes that providing information to rational individuals about a well-designed innovation will ensure that innovation's adoption. This is because it is assumed that it is in the rational self-interest of clients to adopt a high quality product.

Ideally, the innovation itself is developed through a linear planning process that involves a careful division of labor, in which different specialists work on separate aspects of a project. Planning begins with basic research. This basic research is then followed by subsequent phases of applied research, development and testing of prototypes, mass production, and packaging. Finally, the innovation is diffused to a large number of potential users. It is assumed that the high development costs entailed by this approach to implementing change will be offset by the long-term benefits of efficiency and the anticipated high quality of the innovation(s) that are produced.

Although the innovations that are produced in this way, such as new hybrid varieties of corn or, in a language education context, the notional–functional syllabus, can indeed be of very high quality and can also become widely adopted, there is an inherent lack of flexibility in this approach to making change happen. Furthermore, because end users are rarely as passive as proponents of this approach seem to assume, particularly in the educational sector, potential adopters frequently feel a lack of ownership for such innovations. That is, end users have little stake in the ultimate success of these innovations because they did not have any opportunity to shape them during their development. In terms of an innovation's attributes, this lack of ownership is frequently perceived as a relative disadvantage by end users, which may therefore inhibit its adoption. To be sure, the general success of the notional–functional syllabus demonstrates that an RD&D model used in conjunction with an empirical–rational strategy can result in satisfactory adoption rates, particularly in the short term. However, the adoption of such closely controlled innovations is often skin-deep and may also be abandoned in the longer term. For this reason, some of the most influential apologists for an RD&D model/empirical–rational strategy of change in education, such as Egon Guba, have reversed their earlier stands advocating the use of this approach (Aoki, 1984).

The RD&D Model/Power–Coercive Strategy. When a power-coercive strategy of change is used, change agents (i.e., the proponents of an innovation) typically rely on their hierarchical position in an organization to mandate adoption by subordinates. Typically, a carrot-and-stick approach is used to ensure adoption: Adopters are rewarded with financial or other inducements, whereas resisters are punished by various sanctions or forms of disciplinary action. The use of such a strategy is generally criticized in the theoretical literature on the grounds that, like the empirical–rational strategy, the use of a power–coercive strategy often promotes low levels of ownership by users and adoption is skin-deep. In the end, a power–coercive strategy is ineffective in promoting lasting change, particularly if there is a change in the regime that seeks to enforce the adoption of the desired innovation. Nonetheless, it is clear that this strategy is widely used in highly centralized systems of education. The implementation problems encountered by the Malaysian ministry of education in its attempts to diffuse the notional–functional syllabus in secondary schools is an instructive case in point. The opposition of teachers and other stakeholders to this innovation has called into question the quality of the English language education that is provided to secondary students in this country (see Aruchanalam & Menon, 1990).

The Problem-Solving Model/Normative-Reeducative Strategy. The problem-solving model, coupled with a normative–reeducative strategy of change, is widely advocated in the theoretical literature on promoting educational change. Ideologically, this approach differs significantly from either of the two approaches discussed earlier. The need for change does not come from above; rather, the need for change is identified by the eventual users of the innovation, who are also closely involved in the development and implementation of change. Thus, innovation in this approach to social change is a bottom-up, not a top-down, phenomenon and typically involves the use of action research.

Broadly speaking, there are two ways of conceptualizing action research (Crookes, 1993). From one perspective, action research means "trying out new ideas in practice as a means of improvement and as a means of increasing knowledge about the curriculum, teaching and learning" (Kemmis & McTaggart, 1982, p. 170). From another perspective, action research refers to "small-scale intervention in the functioning of the real world and a close examination of the effects of such intervention" (Cohen & Manion, 1985, p. 174).

In both these conceptions of action research, the focus is on solving a potentially wide range of local problems, such as those that may occur in an individual teacher's classroom or in a large CATI project. It is therefore a type of research that is predominantly carried out by insiders (for example, teachers), not by outsiders (for example, professional researchers).[4] The primary purpose of such research, which may draw on the entire range of both qualitative and quantitative methods available to all researchers, is to promote behavioral and attitudinal change in the individual(s) who undertake it. There is thus no a priori expectation that the results of this research will necessarily be generalizable to other contexts of implementation. However, despite its focus on "local" issues, a term that is highly ambiguous (see Duff and Early's observation, this volume, concerning the remarkable similarities in the problems they faced in the Canadian and Hungarian projects they report on), public accounts of action research projects by teachers may well influence other teachers at other institutions to do action research in their own classrooms (Johnstone, 1990). Thus, the ultimate purpose of this kind of research is not only to improve on classroom practice but also to engage participants in a process of "theorizing from the classroom" (Ramani, 1987) which emancipates teachers from the tyranny of unexamined assumptions and beliefs, whether these beliefs are their own or those of others (Crookes, 1993).

Not surprisingly, the development process promoted by the use of action research differs considerably from that promoted by an empirical rational strategy of change. End users may begin by identifying a problem and diagnosing in a preliminary fashion how they would ideally want to solve it. It is important to note that, at this stage, problem identification and diagnosis are often quite unfocused as users struggle to formulate what is actually problematic. This preliminary identification or diagnosis phase is followed by a phase in which users seek to understand target problem(s) better by gathering publicly available information on their problem. This review of the experiences of others enables users to refine their initial diagnoses and ulti-

---

[4]Of course, in the case of the chapters that I have referred to in this volume and, indeed, in the case of this chapter, the distinction between insiders and outsiders is necessarily rather blurred. For the sake of expository clarity, however, it is an intuitively useful distinction.

mately to develop solutions that are appropriate to their specific context of implementation. Crucially, however, these solutions are not solely based on abstract syntheses of the experiences of others. They are developed over sometimes lengthy periods of time, through an experientially based process of adaptation, trial, and evaluation. During this process, users evaluate whether the solution(s) they devise really solve the problem(s) they identified. If they decide at any time that there is a mismatch between problems and solutions, the process loops back to a new cycle of problem identification and diagnosis until a better solution is eventually found (Havelock, 1971).

Notice that, as in the RD&D model, a problem-solving approach to change assumes that end users are rational and intelligent people. However, this approach also holds that individuals' actions and beliefs are governed by the sociocultural norms they subscribe to. Consequently, if people are to make important changes in their behaviors and beliefs, they must necessarily restructure their current ideologies. This explains the rather intimidating term normative–reeducative which describes the change strategy that is coupled with the problem-solving model. According to this approach, then, deep, ideological change promotes fundamental shifts in attitudes, values, skills, and interpersonal relationships among participants in a change process. In the long term, these changes potentially go well beyond the relatively shallower changes that are promoted by the use of either empirical–rational or power–coercive strategies of change. Thus, normative–reeducative strategies can promote very high levels of ownership among end users. However, this approach to change also runs the risk that the changes that are developed will be of low quality (at least initially), because their developers will often not possess the necessary technical skills to research and solve a problem (Chin & Benne, 1976).

A final word about the models and strategies of change reviewed above. In practice, these three approaches to making change happen are rarely as distinct as they seem in the theoretical literature. Indeed, wise change agents will understand the relative advantages and disadvantages of each approach and utilize whichever approach or combination of approaches is best suited to solving a particular problem. Of course, as Duff and Early correctly point out, such eclecticism is more easily advocated than actually implemented. Nonetheless, experience indicates that it is possible to match an appropriate strategy or strategies of change to a particular problem in a particular sociocultural context. These solutions are always contingent on the kinds of sociocultural and other factors mentioned in the where and why sections of the framework offered earlier in this chapter (Rondinelli, Middleton, & Verspoor, 1990).

PART 2: THE PROBLEMATICS OF INSTITUTIONALIZING ACTION RESEARCH AS A RESOURCE TO SUPPORT A CATI PROJECT

TAs in the CATI project are part-time instructors who are concurrently enrolled as full-time graduate students in a degree–granting MATESL program. As already noted, the ESL courses taught by these TAs function as a laboratory for curricular innovation. That is, curricular innovation evolves out of the TAs' own ongoing professional development, a conceptualization of educational change based on Stenhouse's (1975) ideal of treating curriculum and teacher development as two sides of the same coin. In order to realize this ideal, TAs are required to contribute a minimum of one pedagogical unit to a central bank of in-house materials, to which they and their colleagues, both past and present, contribute. In this way, TAs have the opportunity to develop their professional skills as syllabus designers and materials writers while concurrently developing the pedagogical resources of the ESL courses on a continuing basis. As described earlier, the development of pedagogical materials by teachers constitutes one of the cornerstones of curricular innovation (Fullan, 1982a, 1982b, 1993).

In order to ensure a high standard of quality in the materials that are produced and to provide TAs with adequate rewards for their efforts, these materials are developed as part of a final project in a required methodology course in the MATESL program. Over the last 4 years, past and present TAs have produced more than 50 in-house units which are regularly used in the various ESL courses they teach. In this way, TAs receive academic credit for their efforts and do not have to develop these materials on their own time, an important consideration in this particular context of implementation, because TAs have important dual responsibilities as graduate students and as instructors.

This arrangement goes a long way toward solving the problem of how to manage the materials development aspects of the CATI project. However, it does not necessarily promote parallel changes in the development of new methodological skills and value systems by TAs. The development of new materials by TAs is no more than a convenient entry point into the deeper process of curricular innovation. In this regard, it is, after all, perfectly possible for individuals to develop materials that are highly innovative on paper and yet to teach these materials in a traditional fashion. In such a scenario, which is by no means uncommon, deeper changes in teachers' methodological behaviors or beliefs about what constitutes good teaching do not occur (Fullan, 1982a, 1982b, 1993). As suggested previously, therefore, the use of action research by teachers to investigate how they implement their own and/or their colleagues' materials potentially represents a very powerful tool for promoting these deeper kinds of behavioral and attitudinal changes.

Rationale for Institutionalizing Action Research as a Resource for Curricular Innovation

Of course, I recognize that TAs have used the ESL students they teach as participants in their own research for as long as ESL/applied linguistics programs have required research of their students. Thus, there is nothing inherently new about the idea of encouraging TAs to do research on their own students' acquisition of English, for example. But what is new is the CATI project's explicit focus on getting TAs to examine their changing classroom behaviors and attitudes toward teaching. And this focus on continuous educational change provides the rationale to TAs as to why they should engage in this kind of research at this particular stage of their careers.

As already noted, action research is a form of research that does not necessarily contribute to an abstract, some would say, unreal, never decaying and universally applicable body of knowledge. Rather, it is a form of research which can contribute directly to the professionalization of teachers in training for both the short and long term. If teachers in training can be persuaded to use action research to sustain their own professional development while they teach the program's ESL courses, it is possible that they will continue to develop these newly acquired skills in their next places of employment. Furthermore, because many TAs aspire to become curriculum specialists after they graduate, the CATI project can potentially have a significant multiplier effect, in that TAs will in turn be able to induce other teachers at other institutions to do action research.

Thus, the CATI project has both local and general implications. It can contribute to the short- and long-term professionalization of individual TAs. And, at the same time, it can contribute to the on-going development of the ESL curriculum. But it can also contribute in a small way to an important emerging critique of the profession of second language teaching. As persuasively argued by Clarke (1994), the profession is currently organized in such a way that teachers are passive consumers of researchers' abstract theories of language learning and teaching. In other words, in terms of how knowledge is constructed and utilized (see part 1), the profession's general preference to date for an RD&D/empirical–rational strategy of promoting change tends to undermine the value of the practical theories that teachers develop concerning how best to help learners learn. Institutionalizing a problem–solving/normative–reeducative approach to making change happen in this particular CATI project not only gives individual TAs the opportunity to change their pedagogical practices and beliefs through action research, but it may also eventually help to correct the current imbalance between different conceptions of theory and research, and help to put the roles that these various kinds of theory and research play in the evolution of second language teaching in better perspective (Ellis, 1994; van Lier, 1994).

An Example of Qualitative Action Research

Let me now review a qualitative action research project carried out by a TA in the CATI project described previously to
give readers an idea of what this kind of research looks like.
As we see, Susan's project (not the TA's real name) led her
to critique and ultimately change her own teaching behaviors and values in a rather significant fashion. Susan was
using some ESL composition materials that had been produced by a colleague. She first audio and videotaped her
class and then transcribed the interaction that occurred in
whole class and small group activities in two consecutive
class periods, yielding a total of 4 hours of classroom talk.
As is typical of much action research, Susan had not yet
identified a specific problem to work on at this very preliminary stage of her project, save, perhaps, to find out what
really went on in her own classroom.[5] But after reading
through her transcripts, Susan noticed that one female
Korean student, Jesun (not the student's real name), whom
she had initially perceived to be a shy, low-level learner
who did not participate in class, actually behaved in ways
that did not conform to the image that Susan had constructed of her.

Susan's initial perceptions of Jesun were based on a variety of sources, including information provided by Jesun
in journal entries and on a student information sheet. In
addition, Susan used her own observations of Jesun's oral
performance during whole class activities and also her formal assessments of Jesun's performance on composition
assignments. In summary, Jesun's triangulated profile was
as follows. Based on the information that she had provided
about herself, Jesun seemed relatively uninterested in writing. Furthermore, Jesun presented herself as a very shy,
self-effacing student, who was liable to be easily hurt by

---

[5]As the anthropologist Clifford Geertz (as cited in Swales, 1988) tellingly
remarks in this regard: "We are all natives now, and everybody else not
immediately one of us is an exotic. What looked once to be a matter of
finding out whether savages could distinguish fact from fancy now looks
to be a matter of finding out how others, across the world or down the
corridor, organize their significative world" (p. 16).

the thoughtless actions of classmates. These characteristics seemed to be confirmed by the quality of Jesun's written assignments, which initially consisted of one sentence paragraphs that never amounted to more than one page of writing. In addition, Jesun never seemed to participate in public, whole class activities.

However, when Susan analyzed the transcripts of the classroom talk in which Jesun participated, a very different picture emerged of this learner. More specifically, Susan established that although Jesun often had considerable difficulty expressing herself in English, she nonetheless took her fair share of turns during small group work. She also kept small group conversations going by using backchannels like "yeah, uhuh, so, okay" at appropriate moments in the interaction. More importantly, on several occasions, she provided correct explanations of vocabulary items that her interlocutors did not know. She also proved capable of being quite assertive when she needed to be: On one occasion, she frustrated a fellow student's attempt to get her to do more than her fair share of reading during a small group activity, while on another, she defended a classmate from the intrusive probing of another classmate. In addition, she was instrumental in keeping classmates on task during small group work tasks; she contributed in important ways to constructing group summaries of information which were to be presented to the rest of the class; she asked questions during small group work through which she nominated topics that were taken up and discussed by her interlocutors. And finally, on one memorable occasion, Jesun asked a question during a whole class question and answer session that so sparked her fellow students' interest that Susan decided to abandon her lesson plan for the remaining 45 minutes of the lesson.

On the basis of this evidence, Susan realized that Jesun tended to participate much more freely during small group work than during more public whole class work. Furthermore, when Susan reread Jesun's journals, she noticed that Jesun constantly stressed the importance of being stimulated by interesting material. Susan then checked the transcripts again and found that Jesun's interventions in the talk in which she participated seemed to reflect Jesun's own interest in a particular aspect of the topic that was then being discussed. This was clearly true in the case of the question that sparked the spontaneous whole class discussion.

These empirically based insights led Susan to realize that her initial perceptions of Jesun had been inaccurate. In turn, this action research project also led Susan to change both the way she taught Jesun and her classmates and her conceptions of what constitutes good teaching. In terms of her everyday teaching practice, Susan reported that she has become much more self-confident about her teaching and has felt free to experiment with ways of teaching composition that are not prespecified by the class materials. In short, she has become a much more flexible teacher, who is willing to be guided by her students' interests. And in terms of her values concerning the characteristics of good teaching, Susan reported that she no longer believes it is necessary for students to participate publicly in whole class activities in order for them to be actively engaged in learning. Furthermore, she has come to appreciate the pedagogical value of exploiting the communicative potential of students' questions, even if this means not getting through the day's lesson plan. Finally, although Susan herself is careful not to claim any direct cause and effect relationships between the changes she underwent as a teacher on the one hand and improvements in Jesun's performance on the other, it is worth noting that, by the end of the semester, Jesun was producing nine-page papers constructed with multisentence paragraphs.

Institutionalizing Action Research: Issues and Problems

The description of Susan's project given above is typical of the kind of action research TAs do in this CATI project. But what broader issues and problems have had to be resolved over time in order to institutionalize action research by TAs as a resource for curricular and teacher innovation? Three such issues and problems have been identified to date.

The Need to Make the Case for Action Research to TAs. A crucial issue that I had to confront was how to transform TAs' initially teaching-oriented culture into a more research-oriented culture that would potentially service their continuing professionalization as teachers and curriculum specialists. This was easier said than done. If we ask the apparently simple question "Should teachers do action research?" we are likely to get quite different answers from different people. From the perspective of teacher educators, the answer to this question is likely to be "yes" (Allwright & Bailey, 1991; Crookes, 1993; Gephard, Gaitan, & Oprandy, 1987; Long, 1989b; Nunan, 1989, 1990). However, from the perspective of teachers, the question itself is likely to be rephrased as: "Why should teachers do action research in the first place?" Furthermore, the answer that many teachers actually give to this reformulated question is that even if they are inclined to accept action research as a good idea in principle (and many teachers are not, at least initially), they feel they have neither the time nor the background that is necessary to do such research.

In my experience as an ESL program director, TAs' pedagogical values are broadly consistent with the highly pragmatic professional culture of teachers in general. Basically, teachers tend to be much more interested in the practicalities of teaching than in abstract discussions of language learning that seem to them to have little direct applicability to the classroom (for an example of such an ideology, see Eykin, 1987). Thus, the case for TAs doing action research must be persuasively presented to TAs; it cannot be assumed that they will accept the desirability of doing such research as a given.

The Need to Understand Action Research Both as a Resource for Curricular Innovation and as an Innovation in Its Own Right. The problems raised by the prototypically different attitudes of teachers and researchers toward the potential usefulness of action research lead me directly to my next point. Although I initially conceived action research as a resource that would support the larger developmental aims of the CATI project, it became clear that, from the TAs' perspective, action research itself counted as a major innovation in its own right. Consequently, in addition to being a resource that was a product of a significant program of organization development, the innovation of action research in turn had to be supported with the kinds of incentives and support systems that would persuade TAs to adopt this way of making change happen. In particular, I had to confront the highly problematic issues of how and where TAs might conduct action research and how they might then diffuse the results of their research to an appropriate audience.

The Need to Create a Community of Action Researchers. If action research is to count as research and actually result in beneficial individual and collective change, TAs must be persuaded of its value; furthermore, they must be supervised and formally trained how to gather data, identify appropriate problems, articulate their insights, and share them with others. In turn, the need to articulate and share insights between TAs as action researchers logically leads to the need to create formal communication networks[6] which can bind an emerging community of action researchers together (Crookes, 1993). The creation of these communication networks requires organization development. The desired results of this development, the formation of a community of peers involved in action research, potentially provide TAs with a forum in which they may document their insights and introspections for a community of peers and in which they may receive constructive feedback from or provide such feedback to their colleagues. But how is this to be done?

Solutions

As implied earlier, action research is not something that can be talked about in the abstract. Nor is it something that can be institutionalized as a resource for teacher development in a CATI project merely by a project director giving teachers occasional pep talks about its utility. Ac-

---

[6]In saying this, I recognize that teachers have always formed informal communication networks to exchange information about new ideas and pedagogical practices. But change agents cannot leave developments of this importance to happen by chance. Thus, institutional support which promotes the development of formal communication networks among an organization's members is also needed if teachers' innovative pedagogical behaviors and values are to survive in the long term.

tion research must be done by its potential beneficiaries if they are to be persuaded of its value. This position is consistent with what we know about the way educational innovations are adopted. More specifically, as Fullan (1993, p.15) put it, teachers should "behave their way into new ideas and skills, not just think their way into them." Thus, the strategy that has been used in the CATI project described here is to persuade TAs of the value of action research by having them do it. However, such a solution requires a considerable amount of organization development.

The prior experience gained in using the methodology course as a resource for teachers' professionalization in the area of materials development has been most useful in this regard. More specifically, the CATI project's capacity to sustain TAs' professional development has been increased by either developing or adapting courses in the MATESL program in such a way that TAs may carry out action research projects in these classes. This arrangement ensures that TAs' action research projects are properly supervised and rewarded. Four courses taught by two faculty members in the MATESL program are regularly used as loci for action research. In two of the courses taught by a colleague, TAs have the opportunity to carry out quantitatively oriented action research on testing and composition-related issues, respectively. An example of this type of research is a project on the interrater reliability of TA scorers' judgments of ESL students' performance on the diagnostic tests used in the ESL courses. And in two courses that I teach (one on curricular issues, the other devoted exclusively to action research), TAs can do qualitatively oriented action research projects like Susan's. This informal suite of four courses equips TAs with the kinds of research skills they need in order to collect good data, identify appropriate problems, and articulate their insights.

By itself, this solution is not particularly original and has doubtless been used at many universities. However, it is also vital that the insights that individual TAs gain into their teaching behaviors and values should feed directly back into the ESL courses and thus allow the larger community of TAs to reflect critically on how to change the ESL courses (Dewey, 1910; Freire, 1976; Stenhouse 1970, 1975). For this reason, the organizational capacity of the CATI project had to be developed much more thoroughly. In addition to linking these MATESL program courses to the CATI project, I realized that it was also necessary to provide TAs with local, nontraditional outlets which they could use to disseminate the results of their research to their peers. It is this expanded program of organization development that is more likely to be innovative in university teacher education programs.

Note, finally, that the development of such outlets for dissemination is not just a locally necessary requirement for the maintenance of this particular CATI project. The issue of how and where action research is disseminated in fact represents an ongoing problem for advocates of action research (Crookes, 1993). Because the primary purpose of action research is to solve local problems, it is rarely published by traditional outlets like professional journals, hence the need to create alternative outlets which allow TAs to disseminate the results of their research directly to their colleagues.

Teacher' Journals and Portfolios. Teacher journals and portfolios exemplify relatively private fora where teachers may discuss their insights and introspections into their professional development with me. In their journals, TAs systematically document and reflect on the teaching problems they confront in their classes. Journals constitute an important channel of communication between individual TAs and me, in that they allow both parties to discuss issues in an informal manner that is not constrained by the more formal conventions of academic discourse. For this reason, they are a vital complement to the more conventional academic term papers and research reports that TAs also write for their MATESL program classes, including the four described previously.

TAs turn these journals in to me two or three times a semester. In turn, I provide suggestions and feedback as appropriate. To the extent that this dialogue helps TAs clarify issues that they have been thinking about or resolve problems that they encounter in their classrooms, dialogic journals count as a form of action research, even if TAs do not initially realize that this is what they are engaged in doing. Finally, it is also important to note that journals are themselves valuable sources of data for doing qualitatively oriented action research.

As already noted, journals are primarily private records of individual TAs' insights into the processes of language teaching. But they can also become public documents. When the raw data journals contain are edited and analyzed (either by the writers themselves or, with the writers' permission, by others), these documents can provide fascinating public insights into the writer's evolving understanding of the teaching or learning process. As we saw in the case of Susan's project, for example, Susan had her own ESL students keep journals and used Jesun's journal as one source of data for her project (see also Bailey, 1990 and Porter, Goldstein, Leatherman, & Conrad, 1990, for other examples of this kind of research in teacher education).

Teachers' portfolios are another private forum in which TAs keep a longitudinal record of their insights and introspections into their professional development. This record typically includes copies of all their materials development activities, journal entries commenting on how successfully they feel they have implemented their materials and, in some cases, videos of themselves teaching their materials. Portfolios also include any examples of action research TAs carry out during the course of their tenure in the ESL courses. The principal purpose of these portfolios is to provide a rounded picture of TAs' ongoing achievements as language teaching professionals.

As in the case of journals (and subject to the same caveats), portfolios can become transformed from primarily private records into public documents. Portfolios are potentially rather complete records of how TAs grow professionally over a period of 2 or 3 years. Thus, they can become very useful sources of data for individuals who wish to do action research at the master's thesis level. And from my perspective as project director, these portfolios are potentially also of great utility, because they provide an important source of data which can eventually feed into a comprehensive summative evaluation that is built into the long-range plan for the project (see Alderson, 1992 on the necessity for a built-in evaluation component in language teaching projects). More specifically, portfolios allow evaluators to determine the extent to which the CATI project has coherently engaged succeeding generations of TAs in all three dimensions of educational change identified in the definition of curricular innovation; the development by TAs of new pedagogical materials, methodological skills, and value systems. In turn, the results of this summative evaluation will be used to identify and develop other curricular resources that might be needed to sustain the smooth running of the project.

Staff Meetings and Computer Technology. Staff meetings and computer technology exemplify the kinds of formal communication networks discussed previously in part 1. Furthermore, in contrast to journals and portfolios, they exemplify relatively public fora for the dissemination of TAs' action research projects. Staff meetings are held every week so that TAs who teach parallel sections of the same course may discuss administrative or pedagogical issues that have an impact on their classes. Thus, these staff meetings constitute a natural venue for public, face-to-face discussion of individual TAs' action research projects.

TAs regularly present in-progress reports of their findings to their peers at these meetings. These reports complement the reports given in the MATESL program classes already mentioned. However, the TAs' audiences at the staff meetings and in the MATESL classes are quite different, as is the function of the presentations that are given at these two venues. The presentations given in the MATESL classes are formal assignments that typically count toward the TAs' course grade. Inevitably, therefore, the principal audience TAs are addressing is the faculty member who teaches the course. And the main purpose of the presentation, as far as the TAs are concerned, at least, is to meet the faculty member's expectations regarding what constitutes adequate research. In staff meetings, however, TAs present their research as a voluntary activity. Furthermore, because I purposely do not attend those meetings at which TAs are presenting findings from their action research projects, the audience for the TAs' reports is other TAs. Thus, staff meetings provide TAs with important opportunities to share the results of their action research projects with colleagues and, in so doing, to construct a community of peers that consumes and also produces action research.

Staff meetings are an important venue for publicly reporting on the results of action research. However, there is the danger that TAs who teach a different class or who cannot attend meetings for some reason will not benefit from these discussions. It is here that computer technology is a particularly useful resource for disseminating information to a broader audience than the individuals who physically participated in these discussions. For a detailed discussion of how this technology actually works, see the descriptions in Markee (1994c). Briefly, TAs' reports on their projects are summarized on an electronic mail list[7] called the TAlist, as are the main points that emerge from the subsequent discussion. In this way, all TAs are aware of all the action research projects going on within the ESL courses at any one period of time.

TAs have also begun to "publish" their completed action research projects in a research folder that forms part of a centralized electronic data bank known as the ESL Service Courses folder, which also contains the TAs' materials and other resources pertinent to the management of the ESL courses.[8] The function of the research folder is to provide TAs with actual examples of action research carried out by their contemporaries and predecessors and thus, to give peer guidance as to how TAs might write up their own projects. The examples of action research contained in this

---

[7]Lists are electronic interest groups to which people subscribe, much as they would to a newspaper or magazine. Subscribers use personal computers connected to a mainframe computer; they then send messages to the mainframe, which functions as an electronic "post office" that automatically distributes their messages to all list subscribers.

[8]This database is located on the hard drive of my office computer and is accessible via file sharing. File sharing is a technology that enables user A to remotely access the contents of a file located on the hard drive of user B's computer. In order for this datasharing to be possible, the two users' computers must be networked (i.e., electronically linked to each other).

folder not only prove to TAs that it is possible for them to do action research but also go a long way toward persuading them that action research is a tool which can potentially give them useful insights into their own pedagogical behaviors and values. In addition, the research folder provides TAs with valuable ideas and suggestions regarding what kinds of problems are typically investigated by action researchers.

Evaluating the Success of the CATI Project

As we saw earlier (see also Markee, 1994b), the materials development aspects of the project are well-established. But to what extent have the three issues and problems discussed earlier actually been resolved? More specifically, to what extent has the CATI project been successful in engaging TAs in a process of curricular innovation which encompasses not just the development of new materials but also instantiates the development of new pedagogical skills and values by TAs?

   Although it is too early to provide definitive answers to these questions, many of the preliminary results are encouraging. With respect to the utility of action research, TAs were asked to answer a number of questions in an anonymous evaluation of a course specifically focused on action research. Ten out of 11 students who completed the course responded. For present purposes, the most relevant question asked TAs to evaluate how useful a learning experience their final project had been and how (if at all) this project had affected the way TAs thought about and actually did teaching. The most negative response to this question was: "It was a useful experience for me more as a student than as a teacher. It created, I guess, a greater awareness of student opinions in my class, but no tremendous effect on my teaching, I'm afraid." The most positive was: "This project has affected my thinking about teaching and my teaching even before it was completed. This research caused me to ask questions of myself, determine what my objectives are for everything I do in the classroom, and better interpret my students' work and behavior." Of the remaining eight responses, seven rated the project as "very useful" and one rated it a "useful learning experience." The writer of this last evaluation continues:

> it will definitely affect my teaching in the fall semester. I have built up my own philosophy of organizing group work more efficiently in order to promote independent learning in class. I have become aware of a number of variables that have an impact on group work procedures and how the teacher can handle them beneficially. The project exposed my shortcomings and incited self-repair strategies that would improve my teaching methodology to a good extent.

Thus, both the quantitative and qualitative feedback from this evaluation suggest that the "learning by doing" strategy has been successful in persuading all but one of the TAs enrolled in this class that their action research projects could contribute useful insights into their ongoing professional development. Furthermore, as the texts of the two positive evaluations quoted above demonstrate, there is fairly strong evidence that these individuals and indeed most of their colleagues in this class have indeed begun to develop new methodological behaviors and to reflect critically on their values as language teachers. Finally, although we must be careful not to equate the intention to implement an innovation (see the last quotation above) as proof of actual implementation (Kelly, 1980), it is relevant in this regard to note that 3 of the participants in this class enrolled for elective independent studies with me to do further research on their projects. These results suggest that good progress has been made toward transforming these particular TAs' teaching-oriented culture into a broader professional culture that includes the use of action research.

For ease of exposition, let me now go on to address the third (rather than the second) issue identified, the extent to which a community of action researchers has been built up in the CATI project. As already noted, a network of curricular resources has been developed to enable TAs both to document and to share the results of their action research with their colleagues. The available evidence suggests that this network of resources has not only been successfully implemented but that it is also valued by the majority of TAs.

In a separate anonymous evaluation that included questions on TAs' levels of satisfaction with the utility or value of the resources developed to support their innovative activities in the ESL courses, two questions were asked about the resources designed to enable TAs to document their evolution as language teaching professionals (the portfolios and journals). Two further questions were also asked about the resources designed to enable TAs to share the results of their research with their peers (the staff meetings and the TA list[9]; see Appendix).

With respect to the first set of questions about the value of the journals and portfolios, a 4-point Likert scale was used to find out whether TAs agreed or disagreed with the statements that 1) the teachers' portfolios and 2) the teachers' journals were useful resources for documenting their professional evolution. Seven TAs "strongly agreed" that teachers' portfolios were useful resources for documenting their professional development, 3 "agreed" and 1 "disagreed." Furthermore, 4 TAs "strongly agreed" that teachers' journals were useful resources for documenting their professional development, 6 "agreed" and 1 "disagreed."

With respect to the second set of questions, a 4-point Likert scale was also used to find out whether TAs valued staff meetings as a venue for sharing the results of their projects and whether they thought the TAlist was a useful resource for professionalization. Seven TAs rated the usefulness of their colleagues' reports of materials development projects and action research projects given in staff meetings as "very high." Three TAs rated the usefulness of these reports as "high" and 1 TA invented the category of "not applicable" (presumably because she or he was absent when these presentations were made). Furthermore, 6 TAs "strongly agreed" that the TAlist was a valuable tool of communication in the ESL Service Courses, 4 "agreed," and 1 "disagreed" that this list was valuable.

---

[9] The ESL Service Courses folder was not evaluated as a resource for "publishing" action research reports because very few such reports had yet been published at the time the evaluation was carried out. However, this folder received very favorable reviews from the TAs as a means of disseminating and archiving the in-house materials produced by TAs.

It is unclear from the question about the staff meetings whether the 10 TAs who felt that these meetings were "useful" or "very useful" as a means of sharing information were thinking specifically about the action research reports rather than the reports on materials development when they answered this question. Furthermore, the wording of the question about the TAlist does not specifically mention the summaries of TAs' reports on their action research projects. Nonetheless, on the basis of some of the TAs' general comments on the utility of the staff meetings, it is legitimate to say that TAs valued the reports of action research as one of a number of professional development activities that occurred in these meetings. For example, as three different TAs noted in this regard.

> I think the range of different things we did in the [staff] meetings was terrific. I think in the future, the TAs should continue to discuss issues and articles of interest to them. I think discussing TA projects was also very worthwhile. I would want that to continue.

> Presentations, talks with specialists, discussions on literature related to our teaching goals and concerns have been really very effective.

> I thought the presentations provided us with a lot of fodder for discussion and caused a lot of new ideas to arise.

Thus, on the basis of these combined quantitative and qualitative evaluations, I believe that significant progress has been made toward creating a community of peers who both produce and consume action research on the ESL courses and who use the results of this kind of research, combined with the other sources of ideas mentioned above, to change the way they do and think about teaching.

Some Currently Unresolved Issues

Let me now backtrack to the second issue identified earlier, the need to institutionalize the innovation of action research as a resource for the larger professional development goals of the CATI project. Arguably, the majority of TAs who have been trained to do action research have adopted this innovation, at least in the short term. As a result, they have

begun to make important changes in their pedagogical behaviors and value systems. However, TAs are by no means
the only stakeholders in the CATI project.

Of the four MATESL program courses that include opportunities for action research, three have elective status.
And even in the course that is required (the testing course),
TAs do not necessarily choose to do action research projects
for their final projects. Consequently, action research has
not been truly locked in as something that all TAs will do
during the course of their studies as graduate students.
One possible solution, therefore, would be to require an
action research course for graduation.[10]

Obviously, however, while individual faculty members can
change the content of their own courses, they cannot uni-
laterally introduce change into the MATESL program's curriculum. As Duff and Early pointed out (see the range of
issues highlighted in the introduction to this chapter), it is
vital for change agents to take into account the views of all
possible stakeholders when proposing change. In this instance, my colleagues would clearly have a very direct stake
in any proposal to introduce new required courses. Such
an innovation would therefore have to be exhaustively discussed and evaluated (see footnote 2 again concerning the
status of action research as an innovation). Thus, rather
like a Russian doll that contains many smaller dolls within
it, the same kinds of issues and problems that had to be
addressed vis-à-vis TAs would have to be addressed vis-à-
vis my colleagues. However, as anyone who has been involved in the heartache of trying to revise the core curriculum of a graduate program knows, the level of complexity
involved in such a proposal would be compounded a hun-
dredfold, and there would be no guarantees of success.

In actual fact, I doubt that such an option would represent a viable solution to this particular problem of organization development. It would be far less controversial and
more effective to ensure that TAs do action research in the

---

[10]Of course, I recognize that the idea of having a required course in
action research is in itself somewhat contradictory. Philosophically, the
very notion of requiring such a course seems to violate the principle that
action research is a bottom-up approach to change which cannot be im-
posed from above (Nunan, 1990).

four courses that already provide opportunities for such research. Furthermore, the results of what has already been achieved to date in the CATI project could – and will – be disseminated to those colleagues who are not necessarily aware of these developments. The purpose of doing this is to enlist my colleagues' interest and support for this kind of research. If convinced, these colleagues will then encourage TAs to do action research in the MATESL program classes that they teach. The diffusion of this innovation will in itself entail a great deal of organization, communication, and compromise. But implementing such a solution is for another day, and, indeed, for another paper.

Postscript: The Problem of Generalizability

Finally, a brief word about generalizability. The specific solutions described earlier will only be directly generalizable to other university ESL programs in the United States which have a very similar organizational structure and which can draw on or develop the same kinds of resources as those described here. However, we can use the problems and solutions discussed in this chapter as a point of departure that enables us to appreciate the relevant issues and to begin developing alternative solutions that might be better suited to different contexts of implementation.

What should program administrators in public schools or English language institutes (ELI) interested in these problems do to institutionalize action research by their teachers? More specifically, how might ELI program administrators promote action research among full-time teachers who may have received their master's degrees many years ago and who may have neither the time nor the inclination to do action research?

On the surface, ELI administrators face very different problems. However, I believe the problems in this hypothetical situation are very similar to those I faced in the context of the CATI project I described. Constraints of time and energy, issues of feasibility, the relative costs and benefits of adopting an innovation, and the need to institute a systemic approach to change must all be addressed. An ELI program administrator would need to have a clear idea of what she or he hoped to achieve by introducing an innovation like action research and would have to sell this idea to teachers in terms that explicitly spelled out how feasible it was and what benefits would accrue to teachers who adopted this innovation. Finally, she or he would have to articulate a workable plan for developing the capacity of the organization to support action research projects by teachers.

The hypothetical solutions devised to meet the needs of an ELI and the individuals who are its members would be as context-specific as the ones devised for the project described here. Thus, it is to be expected that, at least on the surface, solutions that might work in the context of an ELI would look quite different from those that were used to implement change in the CATI project described in this chapter. For example, it is likely that the program administrator would have to promote the use of action research by teachers as one of possibly several means of enhancing teachers' prospects for professional development and advancement within the ELI. If the teachers' cooperation and consent for such an innovation were secured, establishing a career ladder which clearly rewarded teachers who engaged in such research might be necessary. In addition, the program administrator would have to work with teachers who were voluntarily interested in carrying out such research. Furthermore, the program administrator might have to grant these teachers significant amounts of release time in order to carry out their research. For example, if these teachers did not already possess the requisite skills to do action research, they would have to be provided with appropriate training.

An ideal solution would be to allow key teachers who were interested in learning how to do action research to take a sabbatical so that they could acquire the necessary skills at a local university. If this is impossible, the program administrator would have to be prepared to run short, in-house training programs in action research him or herself or to hire an outside consultant to provide such training. This might well constrain the scope of the types of action research that teachers would be able to carry out, at least initially. It is also likely that a system of workshops would have to be instituted in which the teachers who elected to do action research could share their results with their peers and, through their example, inspire their colleagues to join them in doing action research too. If these workshops were run as extracurricular activities, it might also be necessary for the ELI to offer participants financial or other inducements to encourage them to attend. In other words, it is up to the individual program administrator to devise a program of organization development that would work in his or her own context of implementation. Thus, if nothing else is to be learned from this example, it is that apparently simple changes often hide a great deal of complexity and that all change is essentially systemic.

CONCLUSION

In part 1 of this chapter, I situated action research in SLCR within a broader diffusion of innovations perspective on promoting educational change. In part 2, I discussed (in a way that is hopefully both candid and useful to readers) the problematics of implementing educational change in the specific context of a university-level CATI project. The results of this case study suggest that, while much has been achieved to make action research by TAs a reality, further work remains to be done in order to further institutionalize this innovation at a programmatic level of change.

Like the other chapters in this volume by Duff and Early, Spada et al., and Rounds, this case study has served to illustrate the fact that the implementation of curricular innovations is an ongoing problem-solving process. Crucially, the art of managing complex social change involves project directors in developing and implementing an appropriately balanced mix of academic and administrative initiatives over time (White, 1988). We should also recognize that, in a sense, a CATI project such as the one discussed in this chapter can never be declared to be finally successful. For example, no sooner has one generation of TAs been inducted into an action research-oriented professional culture than they graduate and the whole process has to be started again with their successors.

It is salutary to remember this essential quality of many educational innovations. If we understand how difficult it is to implement and maintain innovations, then we will have a much better understanding of the enormity of the task

that faces language teaching professionals who are interested in restructuring the field of second language teaching
along the lines suggested by Clarke (1994). Nonetheless,
although very significant obstacles exist that constrain the
possibility of achieving the goal of restructuring, there is
reason to believe that this is not an altogether impossible
task.

APPENDIX

A) The teachers' portfolios are a useful resource for docu-
   menting TAs' professional evolution:
   Strongly agree   7
   Agree   3
   Disagree   1
   Strongly disagree   0

B) The teachers' journals are a useful resource for docu-
   menting TAs' professional evolution:
   Strongly agree   4
   Agree   6
   Disagree   1
   Strongly disagree   0

C) Please rate your level of satisfaction concerning the
   usefulness of [the methodology course] and [the action
   research course] related project discussions at weekly
   level meetings:
   Very high   7
   High   3
   Low   0
   Very low   0
   Not Applicable   1

D) The TAlist is a valuable tool of communication in the
   ESL Service Courses:
   Strongly agree   6
   Agree   4
   Disagree   1
   Strongly disagree   0

REFERENCES

Alderson, J. C. (1992). Guidelines for the evaluation of language education. In J. C. Alderson & A. Beretta (Eds.), *Evaluating second language education* (pp. 274–304). Cambridge, England: Cambridge University Press.

Allwright, R., & Bailey, K. M. (1991). *Focus on the language classroom.* Cambridge, England: Cambridge University Press.

Aoki, T. (1984). Towards a reconceptualization of curriculum implementation. In D. Hopkins & M. Wideen (Eds.), *Alternative perspectives on school improvement* (pp. 107–118). Philadelphia: Falmer Press.

Aruchanalam, A., & Menon, P. (1990). Suitability of the KBSR English language syllabus in selected urban primary schools in Malaysia (Vote F Project Report). Kuala Lumpur: Pusat Bahasa University of Malaysia.

Bailey, K. M. (1990). The use of diary studies in teacher education programs. In J. C. Richards & D. Nunan (Eds.), *Second language teacher education* (pp. 215–226). Cambridge, England: Cambridge University Press.

Bailey, K. M. (1992). The processes of innovation in language teacher development: What, why and how teachers change. In J. Flowerdew, M. Brock & S. Hsia (Eds.), *Perspectives on second language teacher education* (pp. 253–281). Hong Kong: City Polytechnic of Hong Kong.

Banbrook, L., & Skehan, P. (1990). Classrooms and display questions. In C. Brumfit & R. Mitchell (Eds.), *Research in the language classroom,* (ELT Documents 133, pp. 141–152) London: Modern English Publications in association with the British Council.

Beretta, A. (1990) Implementation of the Bangalore Project. *Applied Linguistics, 11*(4), 321–337.

Brindley, G., & Hood, S. (1991). Curriculum innovation in adult ESL. In G. Brindley (Ed.), *The second language curriculum in action,* (pp. 232–248). Sydney: NCELTR, Macquarie University.

Brock, C. A. (1986). The effects of referential questions on ESL classroom discourse. *TESOL Quarterly, 20,* 47–59.

Candlin, C. N. (1984a). Syllabus design as a critical process. In C. J. Brumfit (Ed.), *General English syllabus design* (ELT Documents 118, pp. 29–46). Oxford, England: Pergamon.

Candlin, C. N. (1984b). Applying a systems approach to curriculum innovation in the public sector. In J. A. S. Read (Ed.), *Trends in language syllabus design* (pp. 151–179). Singapore: Singapore University Press for SEAMEO-RELC.

Chin, R., & Benne, K. D. (1976). General strategies for effecting changes in human systems. In W. G. Bennis, K. D. Benne, R. Chin, and K. E. Corey (Eds.), *The planning of change* (3rd ed., pp. 22–45). New York: Holt, Rinehart & Winston.

Clarke, M. A. (1994). The dysfunctions of the theory/practice discourse. *TESOL Quarterly, 28*(1), 9–26.

Cohen, D. K., & Manion, L. (1985). *Research methods in education* (2nd ed.). London: Croom Helm.

Cooper, R. L. (1982). A framework for the study of language spread. In R.

L. Cooper (Ed.), *Language spread: Studies in diffusion and social change* (pp. 5–36). Bloomington, IN: Indiana University Press and Center for Applied Linguistics, Washington.

Cooper, R. L. (1989). *Language planning and social change*. Cambridge, England: Cambridge University Press.

Crookes, G. (1993). Action research for second language teachers: Going beyond teacher research. *Applied Linguistics, 14*(2), 130–144.

Dewey, J. (1904). *The relation of theory to practice in education* (3rd NNSE Yearbook, Part 1). Chicago: University of Chicago Press.

Dewey, J. (1910). *How we think*. Boston, MA: Heath.

Doughty, C., & Pica, T. (1986). Information gap tasks: Do they facilitate second language acquisition? *TESOL Quarterly, 20*, 305–325.

Duff, P. A. (1986). Another look at interlanguage talk: Taking task to task. In R. Day (Ed.), *Talking to learn* (pp. 147–181). Rowley, MA: Newbury House.

Duff, P.A. (1993). Task and interlanguage performance: An SLA perspective. In G. Crookes & S. M. Gass (Eds.), *Tasks and language learning: Integrating theory and practice* (pp. 57–95). Clevedon, Avon, England: Multilingual Matters.

Ellis, R. (1994). Implicit/explicit knowledge and language pedagogy. *TESOL Quarterly, 28*(1),166–172.

Eykin, L. B. (1987). Confessions of a high school language teacher, or "Why I never (used to) read *Foreign Language Annals*." *Foreign Language Annals, 20*(2), 265–266.

Everard, B. E., & Morris, G. (1990). *Effective school management* (2nd ed.). London: Paul Chapman Publishing.

Freire, P. (1976). *Pedagogy of the oppressed* (M. B. Ramos, Trans.). New York: Continuum. (original work published 1970)

Fullan, M. (1982a). *The meaning of educational change*. New York: Teachers College Press, Columbia University.

Fullan, M. (1982b). Research into educational innovation. In H. L. Gray (Ed.), *The management of educational institutions* (pp. 245–262). Lewes: The Falmer Press.

Fullan, M. (1993). *Change forces: Probing the depths of educational reform*. London: The Falmer Press.

Gephard, J. G., Gaitan, S., & Oprandy, R. (1987). Beyond prescription: The student teacher as investigator. *Foreign Language Annals, 20*(3), 227–232.

Havelock, R. G. (1971). The utilization of educational research and development. *British Journal of Educational Technology, 2*(2), 84–97.

Henrichsen, L. E. (1989). *Diffusion of innovations in English language teaching: The ELEC effort in Japan, 1956-1968*. New York: Greenwood Press.

Holliday, A. (1992). Tissue rejection and informal orders in ELT projects: Collecting the right information. *Applied Linguistics, 13*(4), 403–424.

Holliday, A. (1994). The house of TESEP and the communicative approach: The special needs of state English language education. *ELT Journal, 48*(1), 3–11.

Holliday, A., & Cooke, T. (1982). An ecological approach to ESP. In A. Waters (Ed.), *Issues in ESP: Lancaster practical chapters in English lan-*

guage education 5, pp. 124–143. Oxford, England: Pergamon.

Hutchin, J. R. (1992). *An evaluation of innovative curriculum development.* Unpublished master's thesis, University of Illinois at Urbana-Champaign.

Illich, I. (1970). *Deschooling society.* New York: Harper & Row.

Johnstone, R. (1990). Action research in the foreign languages classroom. *Language Learning Journal, 1*(1), 18–21.

Kelly, P. (1980). From innovation to adaptability: The changing perspective of curriculum development. In M. Galton (Ed.), *Curriculum change: The lessons of a decade* (pp. 65–80). Leicester, England: Leicester University Press.

Kemmis, S., & McTaggart. R. (1982). *The action research reader.* Melbourne, Australia: Deakin University Press.

Kennedy, C. (1987). Innovating for a change: Teacher development and innovation. *ELT Journal 41*(3), 163–170.

Kennedy, C. (1988). Evaluation of the management of change in ELT projects. *Applied Linguistics, 9*(4), 329–342.

Long, M. H. (1989a). Task, group, and task-group interactions. *University of Hawaii Working chapters in ESL, 8*(2), 1–26.

Long, M. H. (1989b). Second language classroom research and teacher education. In C. Brumfit & R. Mitchell (Eds.), *Research in the language classroom* (ELT Docs. 133, pp. 161–170). London: Modern English Publications.

Long, M. H., & Porter, P. (1985). Group work, interlanguage talk, and second language acquisition. *TESOL Quarterly, 19,* 207–228.

Long, M. H., & Sato, C. J. (1983). Classroom foreigner talk discourse: Forms and functions of teachers' questions. In H. W. Seliger & M. H. Long (Eds.), *Classroom oriented research in second language acquisition* (pp. 268–285). Rowley, MA: Newbury House.

Markee, N. P. P. (1986a). The importance of sociopolitical factors to communicative course design. *The ESP Journal, 5*(1), 3–16.

Markee, N. P. P. (1986b). Toward an appropriate technology model of communicative course design. *English for Specific Purposes, 5*(2), 161–172.

Markee, N. P. P. (1990). Applied Linguistics: What's that? *System, 18*(3), 315–323.

Markee, N. P. P. (1993). The diffusion of innovation in language teaching. *Annual Review of Applied Linguistics, 13,* 229–243.

Markee, N. P. P. (1994a). Toward an ethnomethodological respecification of second language acquisition studies. In A. Cohen, S. Gass, & E. Tarone (Eds.), *Research methodology in second language acquisition* (pp. 89–116). Hillsdale, NJ: Lawrence Erlbaum Associates.

Markee, N. P. P. (1994b). Curricular innovation: Issues and problems. *Applied Language Learning,* (2), 1–30.

Markee, N. P. P. (1994c). Using electronic mail to manage the implementation of educational innovations. *System, 22*(3), 379–389.

Markee, N. P. P. (in press). *Managing curricular innovation.* New York: Cambridge University Press.

Nicholls, A. (1983). *Managing educational innovations.* London: Allen & Unwin.

Nunan, D. (1989). The teacher as researcher. In C. Brumfit & R. Mitchell (Eds.), *Research in the language classroom* (ELT Docs. 133), pp. 16–32. London: Modern English Publications.

Nunan, D. (1990). Action research in the language classroom. In J. C. Richards & D. Nunan (Eds.), *Second language teacher education* (pp. 62–81). Cambridge: Cambridge University Press.

Pica, T., Holliday, L., Lewis, N., & Morgenthaler, L. (1989). Comprehensible output as an outcome of linguistic demands on the learner. *Studies in Second Language Acquisition, 11*, 63–90.

Pica, T., Young, R., & Doughty, C. (1987). The impact of interaction on comprehension. *TESOL Quarterly, 21*, 737–758.

Porter, P. (1986). How learners talk to each other: Input and interaction in task-centered discussions. In R. R. Day (Ed.), *Talking to learn: Conversation in second language acquisition.* (pp. 200–222). Rowley, MA: Newbury House.

Porter, P. A., Goldstein, L. M., Leatherman, J., & Conrad, S. (1990). An ongoing dialogue: Learning logs for teacher preparation. In J. C. Richards and D. Nunan (Eds.), *Second language teacher education* (pp. 227–240). Cambridge, England: Cambridge University Press.

Ramani, E. (1987). Theorizing from the classroom. *English Language Teaching Journal, 41*(1), 3–11.

Rogers, E. M. (1983). *The diffusion of innovations* (3rd ed.). New York: MacMillan and Free Press.

Rondinelli, D., Middleton, J., & Verspoor, A. M. (1990). Planning educational reforms in developing countries. Durham: Duke University Press.

Schmuck, R. A. (1982). Organization development for the 1980s. In H. L. Gray (Ed.), *The management of educational institutions* (pp. 139–162). Lewes, Sussex: The Falmer Press.

Stenhouse, L. (1975). *An introduction to curriculum research and development.* London: Heinemann.

Stoller, F. (1992). *Analysis of innovations in selected higher education intensive English programs: A focus on administrators' perceptions.* Unpublished doctoral dissertation, Northern Arizona University.

Stoller, F. (1994). The diffusion of innovations in intensive ESL programs. *Applied Linguistics, 15*(3), 300–327.

Swales, J. (1988) ESP and applied linguistics: Hopes for a brave new world. In M. L. Tickoo (Ed.). *ESP: State of the Art* (pp. 14–20). Singapore: SEAMEO–RELC Anthology Series, 21.

Tarone, E., Gass, S., & Cohen, A. (Eds.), (1994). *Research methodology in second language acquisition.* Hillsdale, NJ: Lawrence Erlbaum Associates.

van Lier, L. (1994). Forks and hope: Pursuing understanding in different ways. *Applied Linguistics, 15*(3), 328–346.

White, R. V. (1988). *The ELT curriculum: Design, innovation and management.* Oxford, England: Basil Blackwell.

White, P., & Lightbown, P. M. (1984). Asking and answering in ESL classrooms. *Canadian Modern Language Review, 40*, 228–244.

White, R. V., Martin, M., Stimson, M., & Hodge, R. (1991). *Management in English language teaching.* Cambridge, England: Cambridge University Press.

Young, R. (1993). (Ed.). *A systems approach to curriculum innovation in intensive English programs*. Southern Illinois University at Carbondale: Department of Linguistics. *Southern Illinois working papers in linguistics and language teaching* (pp. 75–94).

Chapter 8

The Changing Nature of Second Language Classroom Research

Diane Larsen-Freeman
School for International Training

Let me begin by applauding the editors of this volume. By inviting the authors to discuss the problems they have encountered in conducting classroom research, the editors were foregrounding the often overlooked real-life decisions and "compromises" intrinsic to all research projects, even those in the laboratory. In sanitized academic discourse, however, they often go unmentioned. Let me also acknowledge from the outset the contributions of the authors, their sensitivity, and some might even say, their courage in admitting that they had problems at all. I would conjecture that a lot of problems of the sort that have been inventoried for us in this volume have gone unreported in other studies, not out of any willful malfeasance, but because we have been so conditioned to preserve methodological purism, however unrealistic a goal that may have been. By being granted access to the decisions made in planning and executing research projects by these authors, we can appreciate how inexact and organic an endeavor the research enterprise is.

The editors have charged me with the responsibility of identifying common themes among the chapters and discussing them. I will do so with the help of the letter "p". I would like to call attention to 6 "p's"; problems, place, purpose, particularizability, participants, and perspective. I address each of these in turn.

PROBLEMS

Certainly the word problem is very salient among the chapters, even appearing in the title as "problem" or "problematics" in two of them. And, where one does not find the word problem, one reads of the "untidiness of the data." One also finds words like "concerns," "difficulties," "obstacles," "dilemmas," "threats to integrity," "compromises," "complications," "constraints," and "confounding elements." Further, the uncooperativeness of the teachers or students is mentioned in several of the chapters, and the complaint that teachers do not always do what is expected of them, or that the variation in their teaching style presents a problem appears in two of the chapters. To be fair, Duff and Early (chapter 1) were aware that they were using negative language to describe their experience and they attribute the negativity to their own stage of evolution as researchers, finding themselves advocating emergent, contextualized, longitudinal research designs, all the while judging them by criteria from a more logicohypothetical research tradition. And herein I think lies the crux of the matter. I do not believe it is just these researchers who are in process. Much of what is construed in these chapters as being problematic would be seen differently, I believe, if the authors were more comfortable with certain of the assumptions underlying qualitative research.

The authors are not alone in this regard; their ambivalence reflects the ambivalence of the field at large. Much of the second language classroom research conducted thus far (see Chaudron, 1988) has been of the process–product variety. The "process–product studies were conducted in an effort to identify observable teacher behaviors that were statistically associated with student achievement" (Kagan 1993, p. 135). Such factors as type of questions proffered, wait time for student response, amount and quality of student participation or input generation were all investigated.

Unfortunately, the particular teaching behaviors that have been examined have not always been those likely to promote our understanding of the psycholinguistic process which is second language acquisition (Long, 1991).

For reasons of narrowness of the research focus, its lack of theoretical motivation, and its treatment of teachers as mere conduits of particular practices (Larsen-Freeman, 1991), researchers have come to recognize the limits of process–product research in helping us to develop an understanding of teaching and learning. Thus, the ambivalence of the field is caused not only by our increasing discomfort with the tenets of simple cause and effect research, single truths and objectivity, but also by our inability to wholeheartedly embrace the notions of multiple, contextualized, and contingent truths, organic research designs, relativity, and above all, by our inability to forego the cherished goal of being able to generalize beyond what we find in a single study.

I am of the opinion that the negative cast in these chapters is indicative of the collective foot dragging of the field in embracing a more qualitative approach to second language classroom research. The signs of this reluctance are easy to behold: Journals still favor experimental designs, the 20 minute slot for chapters at conferences is hardly adequate for "thick" descriptions, and so forth. The times are changing, however, and I predict that before too long, the field will be more comfortable with the requirements and characteristics of the changing nature of classroom research as in the chapters in this volume. Hopefully, this volume will advance that cause.

Let me then now turn to my second p, which begins my list of awarenesses of just what those requirements and characteristics will be. In so doing, I draw on the previous chapters for my examples.

PLACE

The second p is place (I would have preferred to call this section of my chapter "context," but unfortunately context does not begin with p, so I will have to make do with place). It may not be so surprising that the need to take into con-

sideration the context in which the research takes place
has been overlooked in the past. For after all, the assumptions underlying the process–product research tradition
really made the place in which the research was conducted
seem irrelevant. With the emergence of qualitative ethnographic research, the impact of situational variables becomes
apparent. Variables such as the social attitudes toward the
target language, the reasons for instruction, the political
agenda of the educators, and events taking place outside
the classroom all have the power to shape the outcomes of
instruction. Witness the political uncertainty in Hungary at
the time that Duff's research on the dual language high
schools was conducted and how this state of affairs affected
student attitude about the instruction they were receiving.
Notice the practical problems Markee (chapter 7) and Kuiper
and Plough (chapter 5) encountered in the process of trying
to conduct classroom research or institutionalize curricular innovation at major research universities in the United
States. Recall how the fact that the intensive ESL classes in
Quebec were considered innovative and experimental aided
Spada, Ranta, and Lightbown (chapter 2) in gaining access
to the research opportunities in the first place. Clearly the
place where the research occurs materially affects outcomes.

In our book on second language acquisition (Larsen-Freeman & Long, 1991), Michael Long and I depicted the field
by a triangle. At its apex, we placed the teacher and teaching. In one of the bottom angles of the triangle was the subject matter—language and culture; in the other, learners
and the learning process. The triangle was meant to account for the major factors in the second language acquisition process.

Clear in hindsight is that the triangle must be situated
somewhere; it just cannot float in space. My colleague,
Patrick Moran, modified the diagram which appeared in the
Larsen-Freeman and Long text by encircling the triangle
and labeling the resulting area "context" (not being familar
with my p scheme). In a paper accompanying the suggested
modification, Moran (1994) wrote:

> Such societal [contextual] factors are critical. It makes a dif-
> ference, for instance, if the language to be taught is a recog-

nized second language in the society, as in the case of a bilingual country like Canada. If the social context involves bilingual education as practiced in some parts of the U.S. where the first (or second) language is to serve as a means of instruction only until students can function effectively in English, these factors will affect the nature of the language teaching. If the language is taught in high school in a community where it is viewed as a vehicle facilitating entry into colleges and universities, this too will affect language teachers and teaching. If, on the other hand, the second language is viewed as a national educational priority, as a means of furthering the national interest, this too will affect language teaching...Also, in certain contexts, different languages are likely to have different statuses, further affecting language teaching. (pp. 19–20)

Although drawing a circle around the triangle may seem a modest modification, I think that it is in the chapters in this volume that we begin to appreciate just how narrowly focused our studies of input and interaction in predominantly decontextualized language classrooms (Duff & Early, chapter 1) have been. As Rounds has put it "Work of these teachers and learners takes place in schools that have their own sets of political, financial, educational and social concerns" (Rounds, p. 45). We can no longer ignore place.

PURPOSE

Equally diverse, but also overlooked in my opinion, is the purpose for our investigations (the third p). It is clear from the chapters in this volume that the researcher's purpose in undertaking a particular investigation is not the only one that counts. We read in the chapters collected here how the desires of the school administrators in Rounds' (chapter 3) study, the funders in the Duff and Early (chapter 1) projects, and the teachers and school boards in Spada, Ranta, and Lightbown's (chapter 2) work influenced the goals of the research. We learned how the language coordinator in the Kuiper and Plough study (chapter 5), and the theoretical, pedagogical, and institutional screens in the Rounds and Schachter (chapter 6) study fundamentally shaped the research design. This leads legitimately to the question of just whose research agenda is it anyway?

I cannot help but note that the answer to this question determines the facility with which access to the classroom is gained in the first place. A striking contrast in these chapters can be found between the comparatively free and easy access to classrooms described in the Spada, Ranta, and Lightbown chapter and the struggle for access which some of the other researchers experienced. It appears that the reason lies in the perceived purpose for the research. Although Spada, Ranta, and Lightbown (chapter 2) were initially invited in to investigate specific questions that the teachers, parents, and school board had in mind, several of the other researchers came in with a set question in mind, and were often greeted with the suspicion that the teachers themselves and their effectiveness were the true objects of study, despite researchers' assurance to the contrary.

And as Polio (chapter 4) points out, teachers have just cause for suspicion. Sometimes it is the case that a researcher's question results in at least an implicit evaluation of their teaching practices. Rounds (chapter 3) questions the reluctance of one of the teachers in her study ("Why wasn't this teacher interested in how we could help her do her job better?") when helping teachers to do their jobs better was not explicitly stated as the purpose for the study at all.

The challenge then becomes how to conduct a research program with psycholinguistic relevance, and at the same time, relevance for those who are the objects of study (including, of course, second language students) and whose issues may be framed differently. A solution here may lie in the third framework of Cameron, Frazier, Harvey, Rampton, and Richardson (1993) to which Rounds draws our attention. With the third, the empowerment framework, "what those you study want to know becomes an issue" (p. 57). She suggests that researchers should take such needs into account.

Of course, it is not only teachers and researchers who might have a say in the research program. Duff and Early (chapter 1) speak of the conflicting agendas when there are multiple stakeholders involved (government funding agencies, ministries of education, pedagogical institutes, school district officials, school administrators, teachers' professional associations, etc.).

But it would be misleading to imply that there is consensus among researchers themselves as to the purpose or reason for undertaking an investigation. It is probably fair to say that most researchers share the utilitarian motives for doing research of securing and maintaining employment, satisfying intellectual curiosity and/or degree requirements. But beyond these, there may be little accord. In the chapters in this volume, we have read of reasons for conducting research which vary from doing it in order to enhance our own understanding ("We certainly have a responsibility to study and research in second language classrooms systematically in order to expand our understanding of learning and teaching" (Rounds, p. 59), to doing it to document learners' progress in innovative programs and approaches to instruction (Duff & Early, chapter 1—dual-language secondary schools and methods of integrating language and content instruction), to doing it to explicitly investigate "which differences in instruction contribute to differences in learning" (Spada, Ranta, & Lightbown, p. 32; Polio, chapter 4; Rounds & Schachter, chapter 6), and to study the use of action research as a resource for curricular innovation (Markee, chapter 7). So, another common theme that emerges from these chapters is that although all the authors address the purpose for their work, the reason that they have undertaken a particular study seems to vary considerably.

I am not suggesting that the field would be served well were there a singleness of purpose to second language classroom research; however, I do think that the diversity ought to be acknowledged. Furthermore, I think it is worth pointing out that some of these purposes depart from the purpose of conventional process–product research which is to establish cause and effect relationships between teaching practices and students' learning in a decontextualized setting. Moreover, in such an approach to research, it is assumed that these relationships are robust and context-free enough to generalize to other situations. In our embracing of alternatives to this paradigm, in acknowledging the complexity inherent in any given research project and setting, must we give up any hope of being able to generalize beyond a given instance?

PARTICULARIZABILITY

Clearly this is a question that has caused considerable consternation to some of the authors in this volume. There are references in the chapters to having to compromise this ideal to accommodate the real. Spada, Ranta, and Lightbown (chapter 2) speak of the decisions they had to make which tended to limit the generalizability of their findings. Markee also (chapter 7) suggests a limit to the degree of generalizability permitted from his research. He notes that the specific solutions described in his chapter "will only be directly generalizable to other university ESL programs in the United States which have a very similar organizational structure and which can draw on or develop the same kinds of resources as those described here" (p. 147).

I would question, however, whether generalizability has ever been attainable in classroom research. Random assignment of subjects to control and experimental groups has always been difficult to achieve as studies usually must make do with intact classes. And now with our newly won awareness concerning the influence of diverse contexts and multiple contributors to research agendas, generalizing from a single study to all contexts seems an even more remote goal. Ultimately, though, I think we researchers would all agree that the fruits of our research should be useful outside of the particular context in which they were generated.

Perhaps, however, acknowledging the complexity does not require that we sacrifice the ability to apply findings beyond the context in which they were adduced. For Clarke (1995), it is particularizability—helping teachers "make connections between the findings of research and the particulars of their lives"—that we should strive for rather than generalizability. Thus, rather than extrapolating from a given experimental study with a randomly drawn population (a rare occurrence in applied linguistics research, but in fact the only condition that allows for generalizability anyway), we might employ a "grain of sand" perspective. If you study grains of sand, you will find each is different. Even by handling one, it becomes different. But through studying it and others like it, you begin to learn about a beach.[1] I find the fact that Duff and Early (chapter 1) report a number of common features occurring in very distinctive settings encouraging evidence of our ability to make cross-context connections.

PARTICIPANTS

My fourth p, participants, is present as a theme in many of the chapters in the tacit awareness that as we broaden the context beyond the triangle of teachers and students, we recognize the influence of more participants in our research. What becomes important is not only who the teachers are and who the students are, but who the researchers are as well. Researchers are no longer seen as objective observers. It is well accepted in the philosophy of science literature that our perceptions are affected by who we are. From the chapters in this volume, we have learned that it is also important to ask: Who are the administrators? Who are the funders? Who are those in a position to influence the research agenda or design?

In addition to who these people are, a critical refrain which arises in several of the chapters in this volume is what is the relationship among them? Notice how the research of Kuiper and Plough (chapter 5) was aided by the fact that the researcher and assistant to the coordinator of language instruction were fellow students in a research course. They could engage in a discourse that made Plough's research perspective understandable and the project judged worth doing. No doubt Markee's (chapter 7) attempt to institutionalize action research by the teaching assistants at his university was shaped by the fact that he was the ESL Program Director.

Pertinent here also is Rounds' observation (chapter 3)

---

[1] I am grateful to my colleague Carol Richardson Rodgers for suggesting this metaphor.

that sometimes unhealthy relationships exist between researchers and teachers. Why do researchers "describe the teachers they study as uncooperative, unhelpful, inflexible, untrusting, and even just plain obstructionist[?] How is it that researchers are sometimes seen by these same teachers as being demanding, intrusive, unhelpful, inflexible, and dogmatic?"

A partial answer to this question may be found in tracing where the power in the relationship lies. When an interview is perceived as an inquisition, we can see why power differences become problematic. Unequal power relationships usually benefit the researcher more than the researched. Notice that in the Rounds and Schachter chapter, sometimes conflicts had to be resolved by fiat, with the more theory-oriented researcher making the decision.

It is not always the case, however, that it is the theoretical researcher who wields the power. A teacher or student who decides to opt out in the middle of a study can wreak havoc on the best of research designs and leave researchers quite powerless. Any longitudinal study is affected by student and teacher turnover and attrition, as the Duff and Early studies (chapter 1) indicate.

Finally, teachers do not always conform to what is expected as the Spada, Ranta, and Lightbown (chapter 2) and Duff and Early (chapter 1) chapters discuss. "...[T]eachers may not always deliver the treatment type intended for their group. They may instead embrace a more eclectic approach to teaching than the one assigned or introduce elements of the experimental treatment control groups..." (Duff & Early, p. 20). That teachers should do this should come as no surprise. They are not mere conduits of teaching practices, but rather are decision makers who have a great number of concurrent and competing demands with which to contend at any one time, not the least of which is their estimation of how much learning is occurring. They clearly have a responsibility to manage their students' learning before their responsibility to maintain the pure focus that the research design calls for.

Spada, Ranta, and Lightbown's (chapter 2) solution to teachers' doing the unexpected is to establish a relationship with teachers in order to "gather as much pertinent information as possible about the teachers' classroom language and teaching style so that the results can be contextualized" (p. 39). This makes eminent sense to me as does their discussion of the helpfulness of establishing a relationship with others in the research community. Indeed, having an ongoing relationship of trust can no doubt obviate some of the problems raised in the other chapters. I do think it is worthwhile, however, to delve into why it might be that teachers do the unexpected. Assuming that subverting the researcher's efforts is not their motivation, why do teachers act in an unexpected or "uncooperative" manner? And why do teachers perceive researchers as dogmatic? This leads me to my final p—perspective.

PERSPECTIVE

Rounds (chapter 3) suggests that classroom researchers need to see themselves "in the same way that anthropological fieldworkers see themselves: as visitors or strangers in a strange land" (p. 50). Although it makes sense, perhaps, to think of ourselves entering another culture when we conduct classroom research, I think it would be valuable to examine more closely why cultural differences exist. "Cultures are not constructed arbitrarily; in order to truly understand a culture, one must probe the functional values of the beliefs and behaviors associated with it" (Kagan 1993, p. 119).

A book I have found helpful in understanding the differences in functional values which exist between the research culture and the teaching culture[2] is Dona Kagan's (1993) book *Laura and Jim and What They Taught me About the Gap Between Educational Theory and Practice*. In it, Kagan, a university researcher, detailed what she had learned from investigating classroom practice from a teacher's perspective. The study was initiated after Kagan had a lengthy argument with Jim, a highly respected high school history

---

[2] Also, they exist no doubt for the other cultures as well—for example, I am aware that funders have their own.

teacher. Although Jim was deemed very successful (as was Laura, a high school English teacher who later joined the study), neither Jim nor Laura practiced "good" teaching techniques. In fact, both appeared to endorse a rather traditional, teacher-centered instructional style. How could one explain the seeming contradiction, Kagan wondered, that "Jim and Laura were outstanding and popular teachers, yet adhered to instructional styles that are anathema" (p. 8) to prevailing canon. Kagan's pursuit for an answer to this question makes for compelling reading. For my purposes here, however, I would like to highlight just one contrast which Kagan entertained at the conclusion of her study. She asserted that one of the basic differences between the two cultures is that researchers see teaching as a science involving a rational, linear process that is best explained by cognitive (read psycholinguistic) theories

> The teachers' views stand in sharp contrast to this objective, scientific definition of teaching. Each teacher's practice is driven by affective, highly personal considerations, each has evolved an instructional style that is inextricably connected with his or her personality and life experiences. (Kagan, 1993, p. 122)
>
> In addition, [teachers] define the objectives of classroom instruction as extending beyond the purely cognitive. (Kagan, 1993, p. 123)
>
> The objectives are broader and include helping students develop self-esteem, social skills, and a healthy personality. (Kagan, 1993, Table 8.1)

I do not want to push this difference in perception any further than I have already. It seems to me, however, that divergent views of teaching such as these speak to why there may be differences between researchers' and teachers' points of view and to the necessity of including teachers' perspectives in our research. Without them, we are denied access to the reasoning behind teachers' doing what they do. Polio (chapter 4) also makes this point. Including teachers' voices should not be done for purposes of social etiquette, but with full realization that without their perspective, we cannot do justice to the data of classroom research.

CONCLUSION

I have attempted to identify cross-cutting themes among the chapters contained in this volume. I have also contributed a few thoughts about what we should also be considering in classroom research. I have organized these comments as six p's. I suggested that the problems that exist need not be seen as such. That is that they are deemed problems because of the field's ambivalence with regard to qualitative research, and our certain level of discomfort in not being able to meet the criteria valued in process–product research. In other words, that they are seen as problems is symptomatic of our evolutionary stage as a field. When we are more comfortable with qualitative research, our attitudes will be different and they will no longer be seen as problems, but rather as interesting and challenging facets of complex situations which we must take into consideration. Research designs will not be seen to be something fixed a priori, but rather will be more organic, calling upon researchers to remain flexible and deal with issues as they arise.

For place, I suggested that we need to do more than give lip service to the research context. We need to appreciate how this context significantly affects the outcomes of the teaching and learning processes. For purpose, I pointed out that classroom reseach can aptly and ably serve a number of purposes, not the least of which is to help address questions posed by those being researched when we are invited to do so.

For particularizability, I submitted that we need not give up on the idea of being able to transfer learning from one classroom to the next. The learning will, however, I suspect not be of the causal variety that emanates from process–product research. Instead, what we say about teaching and learning will need to acknowledge the unique, changing, and complex nature of every context. What I think we need to do in order to realize transferability is to transcend the complexity—not ignore it or attempt to control it (Larsen-Freeman, in press).

For participants, I suggested the need to recognize that many people potentially influence our research projects and that the relationship among them is crucial. Moreover, we must become aware of and sensitive to the power differences that exist among the participants at the outset of our research and how they shift during the project. Finally, I concluded with an appeal to both appreciate and at the very least include teachers' perspectives in our research.

Doing all of this may seem like a tall order. But it is my conviction that dealing with the messiness and complexity head on is far more beneficial than adopting a minimizing reductionist stance. For if nothing else, it moves us closer to describing and appreciating the reality of the object of our study—the classroom.

REFERENCES

Cameron, D., Frazier, E., Harvey, P., Rampton, B., & Richardson, K. (1993). Ethics, advocacy and empowerment. Issues of method in researching language. *Language & Communication. 13*(2), 81–94.

Chaudron, C. (1988). *Second language classrooms: Research on teaching and learning*. Cambridge, England: Cambridge University Press.

Clarke, M. (1995, March). *Ideology, method, style: The importance of particularizability*. Paper presented at the International TESOL Convention, Long Beach, CA.

Kagan, D. (1993). *Laura and Jim and what they taught me about the gap between educational theory and practice*. New York: State University of New York Press.

Larsen-Freeman, D. (1991). Research on language teaching methodologies: A review of the past and an agenda for the future. In K. de Bot, R. Ginsberg, & C. Kramsch (Eds.), *Foreign language research in cross-cultural perspective* (pp. 119–132). Amsterdam: John Benjamins Publishing Company.

Larsen-Freeman, D. (in press). *Chaos/complexity science and second language acquisition*. Applied Linguistics.

Larsen-Freeman, D., & Long, M. (1991). *An introduction to second language acquisition research*. London: Longman.

Long, M. (1991). Focus on form: A design feature in language teaching methodology. In K. de Bot, R. Ginsberg, & C. Kramsch (Eds.), *Foreign language research in cross-cultural perspective* (pp. 39–52). Amsterdam: John Benjamins Publishing Company.

Moran, P. (1994). *Towards coherence in language teaching: The case for a transdisciplinary approach*. Qualifying paper submitted in partial fulfillment for the doctoral degree, Lesley College, Cambridge, MA.

Afterword

This book has presented advice and caution from scholars involved in research in classroom settings. In so doing, the authors have explored a variety of human, social, and political issues involved in the carrying out of classroom research. Collectively, the chapters can be viewed as a walk through a maze, the end point being a successful research project, not only in terms of the research product, but perhaps more importantly, in terms of the process. In this afterword, we pull together a checklist of sorts that all researchers would do well to consult. We divide this checklist into four parts, understanding full well that these categories contain a considerable amount of overlap:

RESEARCH DESIGN

- What is the research question? Which factors influence the goals of the research (funding, etc.), and which components of the research agenda are negotiable?
- Is the project theoretically sound? How is the project embedded in previous research and what areas of study are being touched on?

- What theoretical assumptions form the basis for the use of technology (audio, video, computer), and what are the practical and logistical issues related to their use? (Issues such as time, place reliability, and availability need to be considered.)
- What are the instruments or treatments being used? (Is one obligated to use local tests? Can insider perspectives on the instruments help?.)
- How is the treatment being controlled (e.g., by random sampling, input presentation, time or money)?
- Is the study pedagogically appropriate or appropriate to the particular institutional context?
- What are the methodological requirements? Are they going to affect the participants (e.g., teachers, students, or principals) in the study?
- What are the time constraints, or how much researcher–subject contact is necessary? Are class routines being disrupted or is teaching material being added, replaced or restructured?
- What aspects of the project are flexible? What will be the effect of participant dropout? Which parts of the design are essential? Which are not?

CONSULTATION/RESEARCH ENVIRONMENT

- What is the administrative environment in which the study is taking place? (Assess networks that need to be accessed—who and how.)
- In what ways can the participants be actively engaged, so that they will not feel threatened?
- How stable are the factors discussed in the description of the environment (i.e., funding, political situation, continuity of participants)?
- What logistical preparations (e.g., time frame, site selection, guidance in the use of the instruments) may be necessary for extensive observations or networking before during *and* after the study in order to gain trust, understand particular group dynamics, and continue the dialogue with participants?

- What kind of feedback should be given to the participants? How can insiders provide their perspectives on the instruments? Can feedback from other groups be incorporated into the study?

REPORTING

- To whom (e.g., teachers, students, administrators, school boards, parents) and in what form should findings be reported?
- How are the results of qualitative research to be reported in the research community while ensuring anonymity of participants and setting?
- What discussions of problematics and compromises are worth mentioning in the reports?
- What factors (e.g., participants' perspectives and their suggestions, overall context) need to be clearly acknowledged in the reports?

ETHICS

- What are the official guidelines for the particular research project (research question, site, time frame)?
- Even if all official guidelines have been met, are subjects being treated fairly and with dignity (Are privacy and confidentiality ensured, and are the findings appropriately contextualized)?
- Are control treatments ethically correct?
- How are conflicts handled and reported?

Author Index

Subject Index